Dramas with a Message

VOLUME ONE

Books by Doug Fagerstrom

Baker Handbook of Single Adult Ministry (gen. ed.)
Counseling Single Adults (gen. ed.)
Dramas with a Message—Volume One
Dramas with a Message—Volume Two
Dramas with a Message—Volume Three
The Lonely Pew (with Jim Carlson)
Single Adult Ministry, the Second Step (gen. ed.)
Single to God (gen. ed.)
Single to Single (gen. ed.)
Singles Ministries Handbook (gen. ed.)
Worship and Drama Library, volume 15

Dramas
with a
Message

21 Reproducible Dramatic
Sketches for the Local Church

VOLUME ONE

DOUG FAGERSTROM

krēgel
PUBLICATIONS

Grand Rapids, MI 49501

Dramas with a Message: 21 Reproducible Dramatic Sketches for the Local Church—Volume One

© 1999 by Doug Fagerstrom

Published by Kregel Publications, a division of Kregel, Inc., P.O. Box 2607, Grand Rapids, MI 49501. Kregel Publications provides trusted, biblical publications for Christian growth and service. Your comments and suggestions are valued.

For more information about Kregel Publications, visit our web site: www.kregel.com

Cover photo: © PhotoDisc
Cover design: Nicholas G. Richardson
Book design: Kevin Ingram

Library of Congress Cataloging-in-Publication Data
Fagerstrom, Douglas L.
Dramas with a message: 21 reproducible dramatic sketches for the local church—volume one / Doug Fagerstrom.
    p.   cm.
   1. Drama in public worship. 2. Drama in Christian education. 3. Christian drama, American. I. Title.
BV289F34   1999   246'.72—dc21   99-43099
                                          CIP

ISBN 0-8254-2581-6 (v. 1)
ISBN 0-8254-2582-4 (v. 2)
ISBN 0-8254-2583-2 (v. 3)

Printed in the United States of America
1 2 3 4 5 / 03 02 01 00 99

A Note to the Drama Director

Dramas with a Message is designed for the worship service or special program in local churches or ministries. Sketches are short—about five to seven minutes in length. Stage set-up is simple, often needing only a chair, table, or hand props, and you are permitted to photocopy as many scripts as you need. Actors can be inexperienced, since the characters and lines come out of everyday events.

Some sketches are comical (although that is not their primary purpose), some are serious, and some have an ending that will surprise the audience. All of them carry simple themes. They are not complicated with hidden messages or deep theological truths. While the dramas can stand alone, they often work better as illustrations in a service or program. Not every sketch attempts to deliver an entire message. Some leave the audience "hanging" and in need of a speaker to complete the point. You, the director, will determine how best to fit a sketch into its context.

Know your audience. Know the message for the program. Know your actors. Select the right sketch—and then, have fun! Enjoy the sketches. Build a team of actors and support staff who will value being part of a ministry that delivers biblical principles and truths in an entertaining way.

Blessings as you share the message of Good News through these dramas.

DOUG FAGERSTROM

Acknowledgments

These sketch volumes are dedicated to the faithful actors and actresses at Calvary Church who volunteer their time and talent and have graciously performed these sketches at the "Saturday Night" ministry, each and every week.

Contents

THEME

Christians believe in prayer. They believe it works, and they believe it is their responsibility to pray, not only in pragmatic moments but also out of obedience to God. This sketch shows the honest hesitation many believers have when reminded by God to pray for one another. Unfortunately, prayer is often a last resort.

CHARACTERS

AMANDA: An ordinary churchgoing Christian. She knows all the right answers, but fails to respond to God's prompting in her life. She is not very warm or friendly. She is dressed semi-casually.

ALLISON: A brand-new Christian. She knows very little about prayer. She is relying on Amanda to help her grow in her faith during a special time of need/struggle in her life. She is outgoing, friendly, and very open. She is dressed semi-casually and wears glasses. She has a pair of sunglasses in her purse.

SETTING

Two chairs and a magazine table separate the two characters.

Allison is seated first as she thumbs through a magazine. Amanda follows. They are waiting to see the eye doctor. They do not know each other, yet they soon discover that they attend the same church.

ALLISON: Hello.

AMANDA: *[obviously rushed]* Hello. So, how long of a wait do we have?

ALLISON: *[positive]* Oh, I think it will be another thirty-five minutes.

AMANDA: Thirty-five minutes? I don't understand why they schedule us for appointments! We hurry to get here on time, only to wait for an eye exam of all things.

ALLISON: I'm picking up my new contacts. I've never worn them before. I hear they itch.

AMANDA: *[trying hard to ignore Allison]* Yes, I suppose they do.

ALLISON: Excuse me, but I think we've met before, haven't we?

AMANDA: *[not interested]* Well, I'm not really sure . . . maybe the PTA?

ALLISON: No, I don't think so.

AMANDA: Then it was the Red Cross Blood Drive.

ALLISON: *[excited]* No, I think it was at church!

AMANDA: *[a bit surprised]* Church?

ALLISON: *[putting it all together]* Yeah, I think so. You sing in the choir . . . and have two cute little girls.

AMANDA: *[trying to be a bit more friendly]* Yes, I do. . . . And you are?

ALLISON: Oh, I'm Allison.

AMANDA: I don't recall ever seeing you at my church.

ALLISON: *[positive]* Well, I haven't been coming very long, and I'm not involved in anything yet, *[pause]* but I hope to be in the near future. *[rather sobering]* However, I have a few *things* that I have to work through first.

AMANDA: Oh really? Well, I hope you can get those *things* taken care of.

ALLISON: Yeah, I hope so too. Say, are you . . . a . . . you know, are you . . .

AMANDA: Farsighted? I'm only here for reading glasses.

ALLISON: No, that's not what I meant. Are you a . . . a Christian?

AMANDA: *[instantly offended]* Of course I am a Christian. *[tones her voice down so that no one around her will hear]* Why would you ask such a question?

ALLISON: Well, my parents went to church when I was young. My mom sang in the choir, my dad ushered, but they never claimed to be Christians. At least, if they were, they never showed it or talked about it. We only prayed the same prayer at meals and before bed.

AMANDA: *[a bit pompous, but not wanting anyone else to hear]* Well, for the record, I am a Christian. And a pretty good one, if I must say so myself.

ALLISON: Cool, then maybe you could pray for me.

AMANDA: *[a bit surprised]* Well, have you filled out one of those prayer request forms at church . . . from the pew-rack in front of you?

ALLISON: *[positively]* Every week for the last five weeks.

AMANDA: *[short and to the point]* Well, there you are, many people are praying for you.

ALLISON: *[passionately]* But, I read in the Bible that prayers by good Christians have a lot of power. And seeing that you are a pretty good Christian, *[with hesitation]* I just thought that maybe *you* would pray for me.

AMANDA: *[patronizing]* Yes, of course, I will pray for you. Now the name is Denise, isn't it?

ALLISON: Ah, close, it's Allison.

AMANDA: Thank you, Allison.

[Allison folds her hands and bows to pray, as Amanda picks up a magazine. There is a long, awkward silence. Allison is waiting for prayer, and Amanda wants to escape the moment and finally realizes that she needs to say something as she sees her new friend waiting.]

AMANDA: What on earth are you doing?

ALLISON: *[innocent]* Waiting for you to pray for me.

AMANDA: *[defensive]* But we are in the eye doctor's waiting room.

ALLISON: *[naive]* Great, huh? And we have about another twenty minutes.

AMANDA: This is just not going to work very well.

ALLISON: Why not? God will hear you.

AMANDA: *[still defensive]* I know that, . . . but it's just not the same without the *organ music* and . . . there are no *stained glass windows*.

ALLISON: *[looks a little puzzled, yet eager to make this work while she pulls the sunglasses out of her purse]* Look, how about I hum for you and you can wear my sunglasses. Then will you pray for me?

AMANDA: *[looking Allison in the eye]* You are not going to give up, are you?

ALLISON: Do you think I should give up?

AMANDA: Listen, if I pray for you—

ALLISON: Right here . . .

AMANDA: Yes, right here, will you be satisfied?

ALLISON: That's all I ask.

AMANDA: *[looking around]* All right . . . here goes. *[straight, to the point, with one breath]* God bless this poor pathetic child of yours. Fix whatever is wrong in her life and do it rather quickly, please! Amen!

ALLISON: *[sincerely]* Thanks, that really means a lot. You know, I feel a whole lot better.

AMANDA: Well, I'm glad. *[goes right back to her magazine]*

ALLISON: You know, you have helped me so much that I want to take the rest of our time and pray for you.

AMANDA: *[dismayed]* Thank you. I am sure you will.

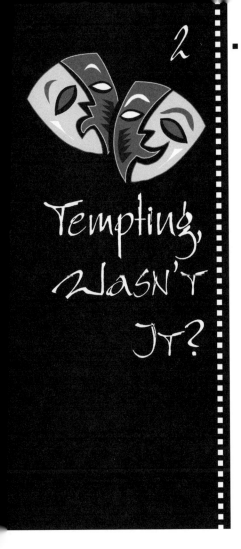

THEME

Temptation begins with subtle desire (read James 1:13–15). Then, it grows and grows into full-blown sin. If not resisted, it concludes with death. This sketch goes way back to the beginning of time with the first sin, no different than any other.

CHARACTERS

ADAM: Our first man. Dress should be a solid-colored sweat suit or other plain clothing.

EVE: Our first woman. Dress should be similar to Adam's.

SETTING

A park bench with bushes would be enough, the simpler the better.

There is a sense of darkness as Adam and Eve come from opposite ends of the stage. As they get closer, a light slowly comes up, and they back into each other with great surprise.

ADAM/EVE: *[upon impact, both yell and jump back]* Aaaagh!

EVE: *[disgusted]* Oh, it's you.

ADAM: *[perturbed]* And just who did you think it would be?

EVE: Well? I wasn't sure. . . . In fact, I'm not sure of anything anymore.

ADAM: Oh, now you're going to start changing your mind on me?

EVE: I think it is a woman's prerogative. Look, just forget it. And don't sneak up on me like that again!

ADAM: *[beginning to argue]* Oh, like this is *my* fault.

EVE: Did I *say* this was your fault?

ADAM: Well, you might as well have said it. It certainly is in your tone of voice.

EVE: You are not going to let this thing go, are you?

ADAM: *[intense]* Oh, like I can just brush this off as if nothing has happened. Look, *woman*, we have lost everything because of you!

EVE: *[angry]* You are just as responsible as me. *[in his face]* You were there the whole time. I didn't hear you saying no, now did I?

ADAM: All right, . . . let's just bury the hatchet and we will call it . . . a . . . seventy *[points to her]* thirty *[points to himself]* split.

EVE: *[irate]* Seventy-thirty nothing! It is fifty-fifty all the way. You are just as responsible—if not more.

ADAM: *[eye to eye]* All right, . . . sixty-forty.

EVE: *[firm]* Fifty-fifty.

ADAM: *[nose to nose]* Fifty-one–forty-nine.

EVE: *[stronger than ever]* Fifty-fifty.

ADAM: You're not going to give an inch, are you?

EVE: We're in this together.

[Both sit down exhausted, big sighs.]

ADAM: *[a little more sincere]* Okay, so what made you do it?

EVE: *[remorseful]* I just don't know.

ADAM: Look, I'll accept the fifty-fifty. What made you cave in?

EVE: I thought it was a good deal?

ADAM: It did sound too good to be true. But why? We had it so good where we were.

EVE: I have been asking the same thing for the last twenty-four hours, since . . .

ADAM: Since our world caved in around us.

EVE: *[sorrowful, withdrawn as if shivering]* I've never felt so cold and scared in my whole life.

ADAM: Me either.

EVE: *[begins to reflect on why they sinned]* You know, I really believed that lie. I really thought we could have it all . . . for doing so little.

ADAM: *[with passion]* I know. . . . It *sounded* so good.

EVE: It *looked* so good.

ADAM: It *smelled* wonderful.

EVE: It *felt* so . . . right.

ADAM: I thought we would have everything we wanted . . .

EVE: . . . and more.

ADAM: I used to walk by it every day and just . . . dream.

EVE: Me too. I would dream of what life could be . . . if *we* were in control.

ADAM: I was so hungry.

EVE: I was so ready . . . and . . .

ADAM/EVE: *[disgusted]* . . . it tasted just awful.

[Both slump with heads in their hands.]

EVE: *[pause]* So, what are we going to do now?

ADAM: I don't know. Maybe we need to split up. We're not very good for each other.

EVE: But who else do we have?

ADAM: You're right.

EVE: I know I am.

ADAM: Look, don't start. This could be a long road for us.

EVE: Where do you think we need to begin?

ADAM: First of all, we need to tell Him *[points up]* what *you* did.

EVE: Excuse me? What *I* did? *[She stares at him.]*

ADAM: *[responds with hesitation]* All right, what *we* did. . . . *[He looks away with a spirit of confession.]* And what . . . I did . . . and what I didn't do.

EVE: Adam, as God leads you, I will follow you.

ADAM: Eve, are you sure? I haven't done very well so far.

EVE: I really believe God will forgive us.

ADAM: You know there will be some consequences.

EVE: I know. By the way, speaking of consequences, . . . Adam, what do you think God meant by *death?*

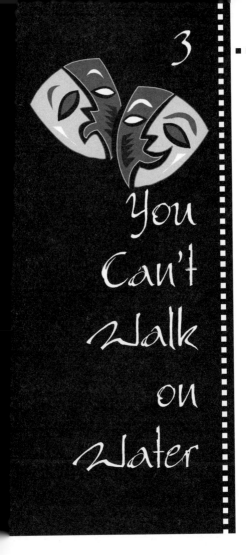

3

You Can't Walk on Water

THEME

The miracles of the Bible are unbelievable to many. However, God's miracles remind the believer of God's sovereign power and grace. The purpose of God's miracles is to draw us closer to Christ.

CHARACTERS

BARTHOLOMEW: A first-century character who is a bit feisty. First-century dress is suggested but not necessary.

THADDEUS: Another first-century character. He is one of Jesus' disciples. Dress should be similar to Bartholomew's.

SETTING

Two rocks or a simple bench to provide a place to sit.
Both characters stand frozen, facing each other. As the light comes up, they begin the dialogue.

BART: *[very deliberate and a bit angry]* He did not!

THAD: *[convinced and just as deliberate]* He did too!

BART: There is no way that it happened!

THAD: Excuse me, but I saw it with my own eyes!

BART: Then you are half blind, Thaddeus.

THAD: I am not blind, Bartholomew. You just won't believe the truth.

BART: The only truth is that you are a liar!

THAD: I am not a liar. You are an unbeliever!

BART: It is absolutely impossible!

THAD: He did it. I saw it and that settles it!

BART: No one has ever walked on water before.

THAD: Not until last night.

BART: *[open to possibility]* Okay, okay, . . . let me get this story straight. You say Jesus came walking on the water toward you guys while you were in your boat.

THAD: That's the first part.

BART: *[softer]* Look, I witnessed the fish and bread miracle. Yes, I saw those for myself. So, I can accept *Jesus* walking on the water.

THAD: *[pleased]* Well, it's about time.

BART: *[loud and to the point]* But there is *no way* that I can accept that *Simon Peter* walked on the water. The guy is a loudmouthed, arrogant, exaggerating hothead!

THAD: Say what you wish, he did walk on water.

BART: You aren't going to give up on this, are you?

THAD: Look, Bartholomew, you can believe whatever you wish. I know the story seems a little strange. But you had to be there. Why, we were all scared to death.

BART: Look, maybe you guys just saw a ghost.

THAD: Well, that's what we thought. But then we heard Jesus speak.

BART: Now you're hearing voices? Just accept the fact: You guys drank a little too much wine last night.

THAD: *[very sincere]* Jesus told us . . . to take courage and to . . . not be afraid. And then Peter—

BART: *[loudly interrupts with great cynicism]* And then Peter walked on water . . . yeah, yeah.

THAD: *[a bit apprehensive]* Well, . . . he did, . . . at least for a few minutes.

BART: I knew it! He went in the drink!

THAD: He did, Bart, . . . but for a reason.

BART: *[straightforward]* The reason is he never walked on water.

THAD: He did walk on the water, as long as he looked at Jesus. But when his fear got the best of him, he began to sink.

BART: So, where is old Simon now?

THAD: He's down by the shore with Jesus. They are talking through what happened last night.

BART: So, what is there to talk about?

THAD: Faith, Bartholomew. This is all about faith.

BART: Well, I have faith. And I have common sense. And common senses says, stay in the boat, dummy.

THAD: Well, that's what I told myself.

BART: So, don't beat yourself up.

THAD: I wish I had as much faith as Peter did.

BART: But he went down! He probably almost drowned.

THAD: Yes, but he did walk on the water and *[reflective]* he and Jesus shared the greatest moment they could have ever shared. Peter will never be the same.

BART: And what does that mean?

THAD: It simply means that to be down in the water with Jesus is a whole lot better than sitting in the boat without Jesus. *[a bit forlorn]* Trust me, I know the difference.

[Thad gets up to leave.]

BART: Hey, where are you headed?

THAD: Down to the shore.

BART: *[cocky]* So, are you going to try to walk on water?

THAD: No, I think I just need to spend some time with Jesus. Why don't you join me?

BART: 'Cause I can't swim.

THAD: Neither could Peter. . . . Come on.

[They leave together.]

4

Not Worth Loving

THEME

Everyone wants to be loved. Love is a gift that God has given to us and we give to others. God's love has nothing to do with merit.

CHARACTERS

MANDY: A young woman who has not learned how to love or be loved. She is hard and fixed on obstinate behavior. She is dressed in an extreme manner, with wild colors, etc. She has come to live with her grandparents after her parents' death.

GRANDPA: Everyone's dream of a wise, kind, and patient grandfather. He wears a cardigan sweater, etc.

GRANDMA: A perfect mate to grandpa. She, too, is all that a grandparent should be. She even has an uncanny ability to connect with the younger generation. Her dress and apron make her look like the typical grandma.

SETTING

A kitchen at stage right and a living room at stage left.

The three characters come walking down center aisle wearing outerwear, and Grandpa is carrying a small suitcase. Grandma has a small bag of groceries, and Mandy is several paces behind.

GRANDMA: *[taking the lead, being positive]* Just a few more feet to go and we will be home. . . . *[enter kitchen]* Mandy, this will be your new home.

GRANDPA: *[trying to be funny]* Well, for only one suitcase, it sure is heavy. I can't imagine who else you have in here. *[bent over]* There, now I can go back and find my back. I think I left it between the car and the front door.

[Mandy flops on a kitchen chair, a bit upset, as Grandpa finds his seat in the living room, and Grandma begins to unpack a few groceries at the kitchen table.]

MANDY: Good grief. I didn't ask you to carry my suitcase, Grandpa. And what I have in there is none of your business. So, do you mind?

GRANDPA: *[a bit taken back]* Well, I meant no offense, dear Mandy. I was just trying to joke a little and make a little small talk. And so I apologize if I have—

MANDY: Save it, Gramps. Let's understand this from the beginning: I don't want to be here, and you never expected me to be moving in on *your* turf. So, you go to your corner, and I will go to mine. Deal?

GRANDMA: Oh my, I do hope we can all share the same "turf" as you call it. Your grandfather and I don't have corners and neither will you.

MANDY: *[laughs at them]* You guys are really strange, you know it?

GRANDPA: Well, I guess I will take that as a compliment.

MANDY: Well, it wasn't intended to be a compliment.

GRANDPA: *[trying to work with her]* Okay, then it wasn't a compliment.

MANDY: You really are strange.

GRANDPA: There, I was just *uncomplimented* again, and . . . I . . . thank you.

GRANDMA: *[trying very hard to be positive]* Well, it is great to see how the two of you are learning to get along. And, Mandy, you can call me strange anytime you want.

MANDY: *[slumps in her chair]* Whoa, I don't know if I am going to survive this place.

GRANDMA: Now, Mandy, do you like walnuts in your brownies?

MANDY: *[apathetic]* I don't know . . . and I don't care.

GRANDMA: Then one half of the pan will have walnuts and the other half will not have walnuts.

GRANDPA: That's your grandma. . . . I think I would call her a little "strange."

MANDY: Okay you two, I get what you are *trying* to do. But it is *not* going to work. I wasn't born yesterday.

GRANDMA: Nope, you were born on April 17, 1985.

MANDY: You don't miss a beat, do you?

GRANDMA: That is one date that every grandma is supposed to remember.

MANDY: Why waste your time?

GRANDPA: So she can buy you a Barbie doll.

MANDY: *[crazed]* I knew it! You are going to turn me into some kind of a . . . a freak!

[Grandpa just looks over his paper.]

GRANDMA: *[conciliatory]* Now, Grandpa, that is just silly. Our Mandy is not about

Barbie dolls or any other dolls. She is a young woman who is on the greatest adventure of her life.

MANDY: [shocked] Wait a minute. Did you just say that?

GRANDMA: Yes, dear. You are at the best time of your life. And we hope to help you on your adventure.

MANDY: Oh yeah, like you guys know where I am going and how to get me there. Ha, that old truck of yours barely got us here from the airport. How long have you had that piece of junk?

GRANDPA: [positive] Hey, another one of those uncompliments.

GRANDMA: There is only one way to help you on your adventure, and your grandpa and I don't have much, but we do have love, Mandy. And we have a lot of love for you.

MANDY: Here we go, . . . another one of those things that grandmas are supposed to say, right?

GRANDMA: I don't think so, because we didn't always know what love was ourselves, until we met Jesus.

MANDY: Jesus! And now comes the "let's convert Mandy" conversation to get me to go to that dumpy church you so conveniently pointed out to me on the way here.

GRANDPA: This is not about church, Mandy. This is just about an old man and an old lady—[catches his possible error] a beautiful old lady—who never loved anyone but themselves. And two years ago we found Jesus, who loves us, as strange as we are. And now since your parents are both gone, this grandpa and grandma have been given a second chance by God to love someone with all of their hearts.

GRANDMA: So, will you give us a chance?

MANDY: Look, I am not worth loving. You know I can make a lot of trouble, and I can mess up your lives pretty good.

GRANDPA: Great, . . . then when we love you, it will be real love and nobody will say we are faking it.

MANDY: Do I have to go to church?

GRANDMA: Only when you want to.

MANDY: Do I have to . . . you know, . . . love you back?

GRANDPA: Only when you want to.

[Grandpa gets his jacket back on and starts to leave.]

GRANDMA: And just where do you think you're going?

GRANDPA: I think it might be time to look into buying a new pickup truck.

[Mandy and Grandma look with surprise at each other.]

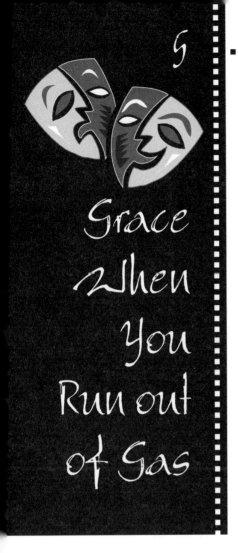

5

Grace
When
You
Run out
of Gas

THEME

We all need grace, the unmerited favor of another, in our lives, especially when we run out of gas. However, we are not good dispensers of grace. Grace *to* us comes from Jesus. Grace *from* us also comes from Jesus.

CHARACTERS

HOWARD: He is dressed in a suit. He represents every redneck in the country. He has a selfish answer for everything.

ESTHER: She is Howard's wife and is dressed up as well, handbag and all. She knows how to pull all of Howard's strings.

SETTING

Two chairs representing the front seat of a car. (A steering wheel is a nice option.)

Music, a country tune, is loudly playing, and Howard is loudly singing along as he and Esther take their places; he in the driver's seat and she in the passenger's seat.

ESTHER: *[yelling]* Howard, would you please turn that thing down?

[Howard reaches as if doing so, and music goes off.]

HOWARD: Good grief, woman, you don't have any appreciation for good music.

ESTHER: Calling it music is a matter of opinion.

HOWARD: Look, I know all about . . .

ESTHER: *[cuts him off matter-of-factly]* By the way, you did bring the fan for mother's bedroom, didn't you?

HOWARD: No, I did not bring the fan.

ESTHER: You can't do anything for my mother, can you?

HOWARD: Look, I like that fan, and . . . *[searching for a reason]* I use that fan in my . . . woodshop.

ESTHER: Woodshop? That mess in the basement? You hardly go down there any more.

HOWARD: *[obstinate]* I like my fan.

ESTHER: Woodshop, huh? Did you ever repair that chair for Mrs. Carter?

HOWARD: I haven't had time.

ESTHER: You have time to go fishing.

HOWARD: I haven't had time to fix her chair.

ESTHER: But you broke her chair.

HOWARD: It's an old piece of junk!

ESTHER: It's a valuable antique!

HOWARD: *[looking at Esther]* Call it what you wish . . . it's junk!

ESTHER: *[looking ahead, screams]* Howard, look out!!!

[They lean/swerve to the left.]

HOWARD: Wow, that was a close call.

ESTHER: *[turning around]* You almost hit that lady on the side of the road.

HOWARD: *[looking in the rearview mirror]* What in the world is she doing with that tire iron?

ESTHER: She was trying to change her flat tire. *[moves his mirror so she can see]* And it looks like she is having a tough time.

HOWARD: *[turns mirror back]* She should have taken that mechanics class for dummies.

ESTHER: *[sarcastically]* Well, thank you, Don Juan . . . my hero and defender of those in need. It looks rather obvious that we are not going to help her.

HOWARD: Look, do I have triple A stamped on my forehead?

ESTHER: Nope, not even a double B, just a big C for—

HOWARD: *[cuts her off]* All right, end of discussion. Someone will stop and help the old girl. Besides, you made me dress up to have dinner at your mother's.

ESTHER: By the way, you did tell Mr. McCormick across the street that it was you who backed into and knocked down his mailbox?

HOWARD: Well, . . . I . . . ah, . . . you know how busy I have been.

ESTHER: Howard, he is our neighbor. And he did shovel our drive last winter when you had knee surgery. And, he mowed our grass when we were on vacation because *you* forgot to hire the neighbor boy. And he is the one who helped you install your new—

HOWARD: *[unhappy]* All right, I will tell him I ran over his mailbox.

[Car begins to jerk. Howard and Esther jerk along.]

ESTHER: I can't believe it, we are running out of gas, aren't we?

HOWARD: This is your car. Don't you put gas in this thing?

ESTHER: Fine, Einstein, blame it on me.

HOWARD: Look, you can just walk back to that filling station we passed about ten minutes ago.

ESTHER: Excuse me?

HOWARD: Hey, I've got the bad knee, and you do the walking thing every morning.

ESTHER: Well, your thumb isn't broken. Just get out and use it!

HOWARD: *[grumbles, gets out of car, and yells at traffic]* Hey, stop! *[pause]* Give me a break, man. *[pause]* Yo, truck driver! *[pause]* Same to ya, pal. *[pause]* Yes, ha, here is somebody stopping now.

[Both freeze. Sign is shown to audience reading, "Ten Minutes Later." When the sign carrier exits, Howard gets back in the car with a rather sober appearance and a very soft demeanor.]

ESTHER: *[curious]* Howard, that lady who stopped with the gas can, wasn't that . . .

HOWARD: . . . the lady I passed who was fixing her tire? She's the one.

ESTHER: *[embarrassed]* Did she recognize us?

HOWARD: *[numb]* Very much so.

ESTHER: *[shocked]* And she still wanted to help . . . us?

HOWARD: In fact, she offered money to fill up our gas tank at the next exit.

ESTHER: What in the world would motivate a person to do that?

HOWARD: I'm not really sure, but I think I know.

ESTHER: Cut the riddles, what do you mean?

HOWARD: *[still stunned]* When I said "thank you," she smiled and said, "God bless you and Jesus loves you."

[Howard begins the action of turning the car around.]

ESTHER: Howard, where are you going?

HOWARD: Back to our house.

ESTHER: But, what about dinner at mother's?

HOWARD: We will be just a little late. I need to get the fan from my woodshop and see Mr. McCormick about his mailbox.

6

The Hate-Free Zone

THEME

We would all love to live in a world where there is no hatred but only love for one another. Can a world like that exist? Well, this sketch tries to make it possible. Then let the viewer decide.

CHARACTERS

MOLLY LOVE: Age twelve, is pig-tailed, bright-eyed, and altogether lovely. She wears her Sunday-best dress.

BOBBY LOVE: Age sixteen, is an all-American and perfect in everything. He wears dress slacks and a preppy shirt and sweater.

FATHER LOVE: The perfect picture of *Father Knows Best*. He wears a cardigan with dress shirt and tie.

MOTHER LOVE: The June Cleaver of today. She wears her Sunday-best dress and a frilly apron.

SETTING

A formal dining table with all the trimmings at stage left and a card table with a serving dish at stage right.

Mr. Rogers theme song or similar music is played. Mother rings a bell and everyone marches to the table with high and positive spirits. Bobby helps Molly with her chair, just as Father helps Mother. Each member uses picture perfect manners. A lot of unison action is suggested. Initially, everyone speaks with a syrupy sweet tone, trying to model perfect relationships.

FATHER: *[to Mother]* My dear, you have done it again. And this is our favorite soup. I cannot wait for the main course.

MOTHER: It is your favorite, dear: leg of lamb with a delicate mint sauce.

MOLLY: I can't wait to eat.

BOBBY: I am very hungry after doing my homework and chores.

FATHER: Then let us give thanks. *[with great piety]* O God, thank You for this food. Thank You for all of Your perfect blessings.

EVERYONE: Amen!

[Everyone takes a spoonful of soup and uses napkin at the same time.]

FATHER: Delicious.

MOLLY: Not too hot.

BOBBY: And, not too cold.

MOTHER: I am so happy that you are all so happy. It is such a joy that we all love each other so much.

[Everyone takes another spoonful of soup and uses napkin at the same time.]

FATHER: Well, Son, how was football practice today?

BOBBY: It was wonderful, Father. I was voted captain of the team.

MOTHER: My, oh my, I didn't think you could be captain and quarterback at the very same time.

BOBBY: Mother, I can do whatever I set my mind to, just like Father.

MOTHER: And how did your play tryouts go, Molly?

MOLLY: Thank you for asking, Mother. I received the lead role.

BOBBY: Congratulations, Sis.

MOLLY: But I will have to burden Mother for a late ride four nights a week.

MOTHER: Burden? Nonsense, I will pick you up when you are done.

FATHER: Why, I won't hear a word of it. I will rearrange my work schedule to pick up my little angel.

MOLLY: Thank you, Father.

MOTHER: Dear, you are so thoughtful.

BOBBY: Father? Did you close the big Adams account today?

FATHER: Yes, Son, your father is now the number-one salesman at Smith, Smith, and Smith.

MOTHER: And sweetheart, you are always number one around here.

[Everyone takes another spoonful of soup and uses napkin at the same time.]

MOLLY/BOBBY: Mother, thank you for the delicious soup.

FATHER: Dear, let me help you bring these things to the kitchen and bring out the next course.

MOTHER: Thank you, dear. You are so helpful.

[Mother and Father get up, pick up soup bowls, and walk stage right to a card table that has the serving dish on it. They freeze as light comes up on Molly and Bobby.]

BOBBY: *[looks to make sure the parents are gone and mocks his sister]* I got the lead role. *[vindictive]* You hate acting!

MOLLY: *[upset]* Bobby, I had to get it. Do you remember the hassle Mother gave me when I quit piano lessons? *[very dramatic]* I'd rather live in prison. *[emphatic]* It's acting class or find another family.

BOBBY: *[sour]* Well, some days another family is not such a bad choice since we are all acting like a perfect family . . . and we know we are not.

MOLLY: *[fearful]* Don't ever let Father hear you say that.

BOBBY: *[apathetic]* So what. . . . Look, he could not care less about me. He just wants to tell all of us buddies that his son is most valuable player, and I *hate* football.

MOLLY: And you're right, I *hate* acting class. *[pause]* Well, at least I got through the soup part tonight without spilling on my stupid dress.

BOBBY: Hey, *[holds tie up]* clean tie. This may end up being a good night after all.

MOLLY: Do you ever get tired of the *same* soup, the *same* salad, the *same* leg of lamb, and the same everything else *every* night?

BOBBY: I hate it just as much as you. But it is all about Father keeping everything perfect and Mother keeping everyone happy. It will be just like this in fifty years. We all have to *love* each other, you know.

MOLLY: And choke down this awful mushroom soup with a smile. *[pause]* Bobby, can't love ever be real?

[Bobby and Molly freeze as the light comes up on Father and Mother at the smaller table, stage right.]

MOTHER: *[upset]* And how come you were so late for dinner this evening?

FATHER: *[defensive]* I had to close the Adams account.

MOTHER: *[angry]* I called your office and they said you went to run some errands.

FATHER: *[loud]* Oh, so now you're checking up on me?

MOTHER: Keep your voice down. Do you want the children to hear you?

FATHER: Those brats? Bobby hasn't thrown a successful pass in four football games. I am embarrassed to go to work. And—

MOTHER: And my daughter can't walk and chew gum at the same time. *[forlorn]* She will be the embarrassment of the school play.

FATHER: *[in each other's face]* And you know I *hate* my job. Why, Smith, Smith, and Smith can just take it and—

MOTHER: And I *hate* cooking the same dinner day after day. *[hands him a covered dish]* Here, carry your leg of lamb.

[They both walk into the dining room with smiles.]

FATHER: *[syrupy sweet]* Hey, I missed you guys. How is our perfect family?

BOBBY/MOLLY: Lovely, Father, just lovely.

MOTHER: Oh, and I am so happy.

[Everyone freezes with a smile.]

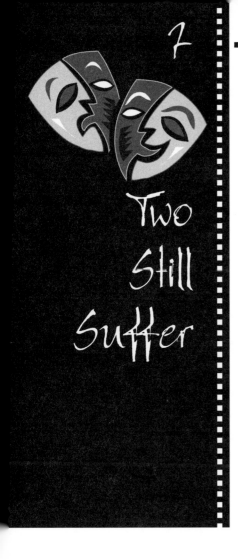

7

Two Still Suffer

THEME

Once in a while we have the privilege of witnessing a mature believer go through pain and suffering, full of grace and hope in Christ. Yet, we must confess that not all of us have that same level of maturity. We find ourselves far less patient in the midst of pain. This sketch portrays two sisters celebrating their mother's victory in suffering and death, only to find their own pain is too great to handle.

CHARACTERS

CATHY: Loud and forward. Her pain from a broken marriage is deeply hidden. Cathy is Karen's older sister. She is dressed in black.

KAREN: Soft and gentle. She struggles with the pain from some wrong personal choices. She is dressed in black.

SETTING

A kitchen table with two cups of coffee would work well. The smaller the table the better, to create a more intimate and tension-filled dialogue.

Soft piano or organ music brings the sisters on stage to the table to share their cups of coffee. Karen is carrying an old black Bible.

KAREN: Oh, mom looked so . . . natural.

CATHY: I suppose, but I have always hated that blue dress the funeral director put on her.

KAREN: Well, I guess that was my fault. . . . I thought she really liked that dress.

CATHY: Whatever, . . . I guess we can't cry over a blue dress now, can we?

KAREN: *[sincere]* Well, I hope not, Cathy. *[pause]* You know, Mom was so strong . . . right to the end.

CATHY: She was a tough ol' bird, wasn't she?

KAREN: Oh, I suppose she was, but *[reflective]* Mom was more than tough, she was so patient, and her cancer had to be so painful.

CATHY: And that nurse had the bedside manner of Judge Judy. Why I would love to take that stethoscope of hers and wind it around—

KAREN: *[interrupts holding up the Bible and leafing through it]* You know, Mom read her Bible every day. *[pause]* I wish I had her faith.

CATHY: Good change of subject, Sis.

KAREN: Really, Mom had a faith that I really admire and envy.

CATHY: What? My goody-two-shoes sister—the one who could do no wrong—carries a little envy?

KAREN: *[rather strong]* I'm not perfect, Cathy.

CATHY: You had me fooled. *[laugh]* I was *always* taking the heat for you.

KAREN: *[naive]* You know, I always thought that's what sisters were supposed to do for each other.

CATHY: See what I mean, Karen? You live in a vacuum. Someday you need to wake up to the real world.

KAREN: *[pause]* So, what's going on in your real world?

CATHY: You don't need to know, and you don't want to know.

KAREN: Well, you could give me *some* credit. . . . We did grow up together, . . . and I think we know each other fairly well.

CATHY: If you need to know, let me give it to you straight and simple. Life is the pits, my husband is cheating on me, my job is in jeopardy, and it looks like we might lose our house in the process. *[cynical]* So, how are you doing, sunshine?

KAREN: Cathy, that is awful. You must really be hurting.

CATHY: I think the new Webster's Dictionary defines pain as: "Cathy Caldwell, 127 East Ninth Street, Indianapolis, Indiana."

KAREN: Cathy, I am so sorry.

CATHY: *[a little sarcastic]* And so am I. *[points to, or holds up Bible]* And I am sorry that I do not have a Bible at my bedside and sing songs to Jesus like Mother did while she was writhing in pain in the hospital.

KAREN: Well, we can't all be like Mom.

CATHY: Why not? You are!

KAREN: No, I don't think so.

CATHY: What could you possibly be suffering with?

KAREN: Didn't Dad tell you?

CATHY: Dad? *Our* dad? Mr. Tell-Nobody-Anything-Dad? *[somewhat sincere]* So, what is this that Dad was supposed to tell me?

KAREN: *[rather humbled]* Well, I just lost a baby I was carrying, and . . . my . . . boyfriend took off in the process.

CATHY: This is not a good time to joke or tell weird stories, Karen, not just after Mother's funeral. . . . Not funny, kid.

KAREN: I wish it were a story.

CATHY: What? Let me get this straight. My sister, *most likely to be a nun*, got pregnant by some guy with no commitment, lost a baby, and the father is nowhere to be found?

KAREN: You didn't miss a beat.

CATHY: *[first sincere voice]* Whoa . . . so, how are you?

KAREN: Well, I don't have a Bible on my nightstand, either, and my faith in God is all but dead.

CATHY: So, what do we do with our wonderful lives, little sister?

KAREN: I sure wish I had some help.

CATHY: You and me both.

KAREN: Can you move up here for a few months?

CATHY: I'm sorry, Karen, but I just can't leave my mess right now.

KAREN: Do you think some of Mom's faith and patience is available?

CATHY: I don't know. . . . Do you think her Bible would help?

KAREN: *[holds up Bible]* You know, I wish I had what Mom had, and I'm willing to try anything.

making God

THEME

God said, "Let us make man in our own image," not "Let man make God in his own image." However, humans are constantly trying to create gods or be their own gods. This spoof is a picture of the futility of idolatry.

CHARACTERS

DEMETRIUS: A "B.C." type of character. A basic robe is his attire.

OGDEN: A friend of Demetrius from the same time in history. Likewise, a robe or simple clothing will work well.

SETTING

Demetrius sits on a stool and chisels a figurine either in his hand or on a small workbench. The figurine could be a glob of clay, wood, or plaster of paris.

Language is played out rather dramatically in old English. Ogden approaches Demetrius, who is intently at work.

OGDEN: Demetrius, my fine friend, how dost this day find thee?

DEMETRIUS: *[delighted]* Ogden, my neighbor and fellowman, this day finds me well.

OGDEN: I see that thou art working on another of thy great creations.

DEMETRIUS: You observe well, this being the greatest.

OGDEN: And may I ask thee what is the nature of thy craftsmanship?

DEMETRIUS: Thou may asketh.

OGDEN: Thank you, my friend.

DEMETRIUS: Thou art welcome, my friend.

OGDEN: Then I wilt ask thee the question.

DEMETRIUS: Firest thou away.

OGDEN: What art thou making?

DEMETRIUS: God!

OGDEN: God?

DEMETRIUS: God!

OGDEN: I see, . . . god.

DEMETRIUS: Thou seest and hearest correctly, and I shall not repeat myself again.

OGDEN: And what dost thy god do?

DEMETRIUS: He can do whatever thou asketh him to do.

OGDEN: *[dramatic]* Can he make the sky fall with rain?

DEMETRIUS: That is not on my god's list of proficiencies.

OGDEN: *[showing great pain]* Then, can thy god heal my tooth which acheth?

DEMETRIUS: Acheth?

OGDEN: Ah, indeed my tooth acheth greatly with much pain and suffering.

DEMETRIUS: Then my god will not be your god, for he doth not remove tooth pain.

OGDEN: Thy god is indeed limited. But can he give words of wisdom and thoughts of comfort?

DEMETRIUS: Surely you jest my human friend, to think that any god could speak or discern the trouble within. . . . You speak not of a god, but of a sage or soothsayer. My god has no lips or tongue and let me save thy breath before thou asketh if my god has eyes to see or ears to hear . . . I think not, and so be it, my friend.

OGDEN: If thy greatest creation of a god is not able to bring rain or heal pain, and if he is unable to speak, see, or hear, . . . then why hast thou created such an object?

DEMETRIUS: Luck, my friend. The answer is luck.

OGDEN: And why do we need such luck?

DEMETRIUS: To charm our souls and give us something to hope in and, of course, something great to blame when all is wrong . . . like thy aching tooth.

OGDEN: But I desire a god who can make rain, remove pain, discern my thoughts, see my need, and answer my plea.

DEMETRIUS: As you dream, my friend. You live not in the present, but in a stone age of uncivilized dreamers with passions for a god who does not or cannot exist. We are left on our own to make god in our image—in our thinking—a god who will do what we ask him to do.

OGDEN: But your god does nothing!

DEMETRIUS: Nothing . . . but bring luck. For luck is the greatest of all possessions. We wish for luck upon one another and asking for luck is one of our most common prayers and benedictions. My god will bring thee the luck you desire. So, good luck, my friend.

OGDEN: But luck is not what I need. I need answers to my questions. I need one who will listen and speak and guarantee hope for today and tomorrow.

DEMETRIUS: I have one thing to say to thy request.

OGDEN: And I am waiting to hear thy wisdom.

DEMETRIUS: To find a god who *listens* and *speaks* and *sees* all that you do . . . *[he holds his god up to Ogden]* my friend, I can only say to thee, good luck.

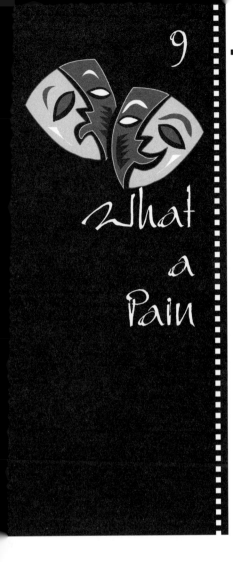

9

What a Pain

THEME

Every day, people go through much pain in their lives. Some pain is necessary, other pain is not. But, regardless of the source or severity of pain, there is only One who can remove the pain and bring new joy and hope. However, even when God does heal and remove our pain, it is sometimes hard to let go of our old ways of life.

CHARACTERS

NARRATOR: Can be a male or female voice.

JOE: A selfish, lazy whiner. He is in constant pain. He wears a heavy, clunky necklace, has a few small pebbles in one of his shoes, carries a knapsack full of bricks on his back, and walks with a cane.

DR. MOREBUCKS: Selfish and in the profession for the money. He couldn't care less about Joe as a person or about his suffering. He speaks with a German accent.

FRIEND: Represents the person of Jesus Christ who has come into our lives to make a difference.

SETTING

Stage right is Joe's den at home. An easy chair with pillow, end table, and TV set comprise the "comfortable" place for Joe in his pain. Stage left is a very basic doctor's office with a TV set. A sign reading "Dr. Morebucks" could be used on a door or desk.

SCENE 1

Joe hobbles out onto the platform with his back bent over. He is wearing a knapsack and uses a cane as the narrator begins.

NARRATOR: *[very sincere]* Once upon a time there was a man named Joe.

JOE: *[to audience]* Yes, I am Joe, and quit staring at me. Mind your own business.

NARRATOR: Ah, Joe was a man in a lot of pain. His foot hurt very much.

[Joe is now in his easy chair.]

JOE: *[groaning and complaining]* There, I will just have to stay right here and endure the pain.

NARRATOR: Joe also had a very sore finger. So, it was difficult for Joe to do the things that everyone else took for granted. Joe could not do the things that most men were able to do.

JOE: *[sagging in his chair and looking rather pathetic, strains to "yell" to his wife]* Dear, would you please come here and touch the remote control for me and tune in my favorite program? I would do it, but my finger is so sore.

NARRATOR: With his sore neck, Joe could not see some of the things that others could see.

JOE: *[calling to offstage wife]* And would you please turn the TV set for me, so I can see my favorite program?

NARRATOR: And Joe had a very sore back and could not lift what most other men his age could lift.

JOE: *[sickly]* Sweetheart, would you bring me an iced tea when you come? I just can't lift the glass when it has ice in it. And turn up the volume when you get here. I want to be able to hear the music at _____ *[insert name of your program].*

SCENE 2

Joe hobbles his way to the doctor's office.

DOCTOR: Vel, vat is your problem. Come on in, you vimp. I don't have all day. Come, come, come.

JOE: *[trying for sympathy]* Well, Doc, it's my foot, finger, neck, and back. They hurt all the time.

DOCTOR: *[while watching TV]* So?

JOE: So? What do you mean "So?" Fix me, Doc, I hurt.

DOCTOR: Look, I don't fix anyvon. If you vant to be fixed, then you need to go to a repairman. Hey, the _____ *[name a sports team]* just pulled ahead, how about that!

JOE: Doc, I beg you, get me out of my misery.

DOCTOR: Vel, I vould love to but I think they vould put me in jail for committing such a crime.

JOE: *[in great pain, yells]* Doc!

DOCTOR: Not so loud, I vill miss the score. *[pause]* All right . . . enough you big baby. *[Doc looks at foot, finger, neck, and back by tapping, listening with a stethoscope, and doing other "odd" examining routines. Each time the doc examines one area his response is:]* I can't find anything vrong with you. *[Then he says:]* Just pay the receptionist as you leave.

JOE: *[irate]* Pay? You didn't help me one bit. I still hurt. Pay for what?

DOCTOR: For my new TV set, vat else, you numskull.

SCENE 3

Joe is back in his easy chair.

FRIEND: *[walks up behind Joe, touches his shoulder, and speaks kindly]* Hi Joe.

JOE: *[jumps]* Whoa, who are you?

FRIEND: Your friend, Joe, your best friend. Have you forgotten already?

JOE: Aahhh . . . how did you g . . . g . . . get in here?

FRIEND: Joe, you let me in.

JOE: *[puzzled]* I did? When did I . . . *[realizing who this is]* Oh, I know you! I met you about a year ago. Well, how are you? You look great.

FRIEND: I'm fine, Joe, but you don't look so good. Care to talk about it?

JOE: *[slouches in chair and scowls]* Nah! Besides, what do you know about pain?

FRIEND: Believe me, Joe, I know a lot about pain. Here, let me take a look. *[Friend takes Joe's finger and examines it.]* Joe, you have a small sliver in this finger. Would you like me to take it out?

JOE: Yes! Please do! But wait—who's going to push the button on the remote for me? . . . Oh, all right. Take it out.

FRIEND: *[pulls it out and puts it in his own finger]* There, that should take care of that. Now what about your foot? *[takes off Joe's shoe and dumps out the pebbles]* Here's the problem. These stones are small, but they can really hurt when they have been there for a long time. I'll just take care of those for you. *[puts them in his own shoe then looks at Joe's necklace]* This necklace is rather heavy and clunky. It's causing your sore neck. Would you like me to take it from you?

JOE: Well, my neck *has* been killing me. But who will turn the TV for me if my neck doesn't hurt anymore? . . . Oh, all right. Please take the necklace.

FRIEND: *[takes necklace and puts it around his own neck then looks into knapsack and pulls out some bricks]* Joe, these heavy items that you have been carrying around are causing your sore back. Would you like me to take them from you?

JOE: Yes, please take them. But wait, can I keep a few? *[They look at each other with disapproval.]* Okay . . . take them all. *[Friend takes bricks out of the knapsack, and Joe stands up and stretches.]* Hey, thanks! You know, I really feel great!

FRIEND: *[begins to walk away bent over, carrying bricks, limping, and holding his finger]* You're welcome, Joe. You're welcome.

[Joe is left with an expression of amazement and gratitude.]

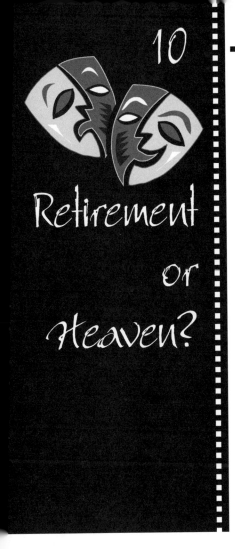

10

Retirement or Heaven?

THEME

Life on earth only goes around once; however, life in heaven is forever. As two friends consider what heaven is going to be like, they sound as if they are planning a new retirement home.

CHARACTERS

LESTER: Age eighty, has had a wonderful life on earth. He is apprehensive about his "new" life in heaven. He cannot imagine that eternity will be better than life on earth. His spirit is rather negative. He uses a cane as a prop.

ELMER: Age eighty, has had a rough life. Every pain imaginable has been his plight. For Elmer, "heaven can't wait." He is positive and can't wait to leave for his "journey." He carries a brochure and is wearing a hat.

SETTING

An old-fashioned park bench or a couch.

*As some soft music plays—an old hymn would work—both characters
slowly walk out and find their places on the bench or couch.*

ELMER: *[with eighty-year-old excitement]* Look at this brochure, Lester. It describes the place where we are going. It sounds great. Boy, oh, boy, I can't wait. I have been planning on this for a long time.

LESTER: I told you not to talk to me about this, Elmer. Life has been good, and I don't know how it is going to get much better. I told you, I just want to stay here. *[shouts]* I like it here! Read my gums.

ELMER: All right, I'm not deaf . . . at least not totally. But you must be nuts! I would think you would be happy to get away from these terrible winters. No more shoveling snow and wearing that scratchy, long wool underwear. *[Note: these lines may be adapted according to geography.]*

LESTER: Well, I kind of like shoveling snow. And if I itch I will scratch, thank you. Besides, I will miss having to take care of my garden. Now what does it say in there about having a garden? *[Elmer is flipping through the brochure.]* Nothing . . . right? What a drag. I even heard there won't be any pets. Now that doesn't make any sense.

ELMER: *[looking at brochure]* Hey, look at this! They have a choir we can join. Now that's for me!

LESTER: Good for you. You just sing your lungs out, Elmer. You know I hate music, especially choirs. Now, anything in there about a good rock and roll band?

ELMER: Let me see, it says trumpets, drums, harps—

LESTER: *[cuts him off]* I'm sure you won't find a thing.

ELMER: Give me a break, you old coot. Give me time, I'll find your rock band. Rock and roll . . . you are still going through your mid-life eighties. When are you going to grow up?

LESTER: Don't have to, Elmer. Don't have to.

ELMER: You know, one of these days we are both going to—

LESTER: *[cuts him off]* Don't you say it, old man. Bite your tongue . . . if you got the teeth.

ELMER: Hey, look at this! A lot of our friends are going to be there. *[reflective, with big smile]* Oh, I haven't see Martha in about . . . *[counts fingers]* six years now. I'll bet she looks better than she ever did.

LESTER: You are just a big dreamer, Elmer. *[shouts in his ear]* A dreamer!

ELMER: *[reading brochure]* Says here that there will be no more sickness and no more crying.

LESTER: Give it up, old man. You make this place sound better than Disneyland. You can believe that travel guide all you want. But I just don't buy all that stuff. Look, you only go around once. So, enjoy it here and now.

ELMER: Well this "one time around" wasn't so good for me. There was a lot of pain and heartache in my family. The all-American dream didn't quite come together for me, like it did for you.

LESTER: Fate, Elmer, fate! That is just how the cards were dealt. I got a good hand. I'm sorry about your hand.

ELMER: You can call it fate, Lester. I call it faith now. Just *think [reflective, slowly begins to fade]* no more pain or tears . . . just a wonderful life forever . . . *[Elmer's head goes back as he dies quietly on bench.]*

LESTER: *[checks on Elmer to see that he has died; closes Elmer's eyelids and pulls Elmer's hat over his face]* Well you old man, you just had to do it, didn't you? Well, I hope you made it. It sure sounded good. I wish I could believe like you. *[looks at Elmer]* Say hello to Martha for me. *[walks off stage; light fades out on Elmer on park bench]*

THEME

We all experience failure. We all deal with it in different ways. Our fictional characters are known for their failures, fears, hurts, and losses. They try to deal with their difficulties much like we do, but without God there are no real answers.

CHARACTERS

SIR REGINALD ALLOUWISHES VANDYKE III: "Humpty Dumpty" is very prim and proper. He speaks with an English accent. He could wear a suit and tie.

BETTY ANN LEPEEP: "Bo Peep" is a down-to-earth and down-in-the-dumps shepherdess. She is storybook all the way, with a frilly dress and a shepherd's crook.

FLORA FLORSHEIM: "Old Woman in the Shoe" is a victim of bad press and is highly stressed-out. Her hair is in curlers, and she is dressed in a housecoat, apron, etc. She is not necessarily an old person.

JONATHAN "JACK" HORNER: Hates Christmas and can't stand eating pie. He has a huge ego and lives in total denial. He has a large medical wrap around his thumb, and his head is bandaged. He is always late. His costume includes knickers/shorts with suspenders.

DOC: The group therapist who has the responsibility to help this dysfunctional group of "failures." He wears a white coat and carries a clipboard.

SETTING

Scene 1: A park bench with a bus stop sign.
Scene 2: A half circle of chairs to represent the group therapy session.

SCENE 1

Humpty Dumpty walks out to the bus stop, looks at his watch, and stands reading his newspaper. Bo Peep comes in, dragging her crook, and sits on the bench with a huge sigh of frustration. She nervously looks around and under the bench. It is obvious she has lost something.

BO PEEP: *[clears her throat]* Excuse me. *[louder]* Excuse me.

HUMPTY: Yes, and what is the bother?

BO PEEP: *[forlorn]* Well, I have lost my sheep, and I don't know where to find them.

47

HUMPTY: *[not sympathetic]* Well, if I see any stray sheep, you will be the first to know. Now please pursue your endeavor with a little less noise.

[Mrs. Shoe is making her way to the bench.]

BO PEEP: *[to herself]* What a grump! *[to Mrs. Shoe]* Oh, hello.

MRS. SHOE: Oh, my aching feet. But I am glad to be away from those kids and that dump of a shoe we live in.

BO PEEP: Excuse me, but did you see any stray sheep down the street over there? *[She points in the direction from which Mrs. Shoe arrived.]*

MRS. SHOE: *[whining]* Look, kid, the only thing I see is a pile of laundry. I cook broth all day. I have so many kids. I don't know what to do.

BO PEEP: I'm sorry. By the way, my name is Betty, Betty Ann LePeep, my friends call me Little Bo Peep.

MRS. SHOE: Florsheim's the name, like in the shoe. Flora Florsheim. Sorry about your sheep, kid.

[Jack Horner comes running on stage, huffing and puffing.]

JACK HORNER: *[worried]* Hey, has the bus come yet?

HUMPTY: *[sarcastically]* Do you see a bus?

JACK HORNER: *[sarcastically]* Well, excuse me!

BO PEEP: Oh, don't mind him. He's just a humpty grumpy.

HUMPTY: *[to Jack]* The name is Sir Reginald Allouwishes VanDyke the Third. *[to Bo Peep]* And your mother should have taught you better than to call people names. I am sick and tired of people calling me Humpty Dumpty. I am starting to develop a bit of a complex, now if you would kindly—

JACK HORNER: *[cuts him off]* Get a grip, pal. *[Humpty Dumpty goes back to his paper.]* Has anyone seen a girl running through here with a pail of water? Her name is Jill, and I really need to find her. You see, I have this head injury, and I am suffering from amnesia, and she is the only one who could—

BO PEEP: Hey, maybe *she* knows where my sheep are!

[Mrs. Shoe, Humpty, and Jack Horner start talking at once.]

MRS. SHOE: Sheep. Who needs sheep? I need some sleep. . . .

HUMPTY: Would you please quiet down . . . ?

JACK HORNER: Look, I really need to find Jill. . . .

HUMPTY: *[breaks in and yells]* Quiet, the bus is here!

EVERYONE: *[Note: Optional line.]* For _____ *[name of your program].*

SCENE 2

Characters come in one at a time and find their places in the half circle. The audience should be able to read a sign, "Group Therapy Session Today." The first into the room is Bo Peep. She is dragging her crook and looking rather sad. She finds her seat and is followed by Humpty Dumpty.

BO PEEP: *[friendly]* Hi, my name is Betty Ann LePeep and my friends call me Little *[She slows down, realizing who she is talking to.]* . . . Bo . . . Oh, hi again. Are *you* in my group?

HUMPTY: Young maiden with the lost sheep, it is quite obvious and there is no mistake, this is *my* group and not yours. You, Little Peep, cannot possibly be in *my* group.

MRS. SHOE: *[entering]* Hey, Little Bo, how is the lost sheep department?

BO PEEP: Not so good. How are your million kids doing?

MRS. SHOE: *[extra positive]* Well, Little Bo, that's why we're here. Get all that stuff out in the open and get fixed up to face the big bad world. We losers have to stick together. That's what Mother Goose always said.

HUMPTY: Speak for yourself, Mrs. Shoe. That old goose doesn't know diddly about our lives and what we have to go through. She created us and then left us alone. Our lives are a dirty trick played by someone we can't even talk to.

JACK HORNER: *[comes racing in]* Hey folks, I'm not late, am I? Boy the elevator is crowded. Hey, has anyone seen Jill? You know, the girl with the pail of water?

DOC: *[while walking in looking at clipboard]* Jack, Jack, Jack, are you still trying to figure out where Jill is? Give it up, Jack. It's the past! Let go of it. You can't bring her or the pail of water back. *[to the group]* Now group, so glad you are here. What can we talk about today?

BO PEEP: *[begins to sob]* I can't find my sheep. I feel like such a failure.

DOC: *[coldly]* And of course you are! Anyone else? What would you like to talk about?

HUMPTY: I am sick and tired of being called Humpty Dumpty. When are people going to realize that I, Sir Reginald Allouwishes VanDyke the Third, am a member of the royal household of England? All of the king's horses and all of the king's men are at my beckoning call.

DOC: Thank you, Humpty, so glad you are here.

HUMPTY: Well, of all the . . . [puffs and folds his arms and looks angry]

DOC: By the way, don't fall off your chair and hurt yourself. Now, does anyone else have something they would like to share?

MRS. SHOE: I'm under a lot of stress. It is not easy living in a shoe. I have too many kids and not enough broth. I have too many to discipline and not enough bread. The neighbors are calling social services because I spank my kids soundly and send them to bed. Doc, what is a mother to do?

DOC: Well, first of all, I would try to find Mr. Shoe, and then you need to get out of the house more often. . . . Have you considered a bowling league?

JACK HORNER: Doc, . . . ah, Doc?

DOC: [dismayed] Yes, Jack, what is it this week? Last week you got your thumb stuck in a plumb. Or are you still upset about sitting in the corner at Christmas? Now, I already reminded you to just forget about Jill.

JACK HORNER: Well, she did take my pail of water. Tripped me at the well so that I took this nasty fall and bruised my head. I feel like such a loser. Doc, what can I do?

DOC: Get a grip, Jack, get a grip! [to the group] Today our session is on the spiritual area of life. Have any of you ever thought about where God fits into your lives? [Everyone looks puzzled, shirks shoulders, etc.] You know, the big guy upstairs.

BO PEEP: Does he know where my sheep are?

DOC: [stuttering] Well, I suppose, maybe . . .

BO PEEP: Well, if he doesn't, then I'm not interested.

HUMPTY: [to Mrs. Shoe] I'm not talking to that fruitcake anymore. [points to Doc]

MRS. SHOE: Doc, I heard about this God once . . . I think.

JACK HORNER: Does he have a long white beard?

BO PEEP: Sorry, Doc . . .

EVERYONE: . . . he is not in our storybook.

BO PEEP: Mother Goose never said a word about God.

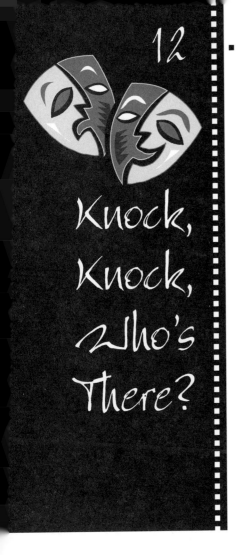

12

Knock, Knock, Who's There?

THEME

The popular sentiment among many people is, "Certainly God would not stop good people from going to heaven, would He?" However, the Bible is clear on the answer to this eternal question and concern. Our characters in this drama each face the answer.

CHARACTERS

ANGEL: A celestial being dressed in white. She/he is carrying a large notebook with many pages in it.

BOB: A loudmouthed salesman, with all the "right" answers to life.

MRS. IMA SWEETHEART: Just that, an eighty-year-old sweetheart. She is the kindest person in the world. It is just so obvious that she should go to heaven. She has been so good. She walks with a cane.

JEFF: A humble sinner who made a simple decision several months ago to invite Jesus Christ into his life.

SETTING

The set is heaven's entrance and can be as simple as a stand or podium with a notebook on it.

DIRECTOR'S NOTE: This drama is written in three short scenes. They can be used separately with music/program breaks or consecutively.

SCENE 1

Angel is at the podium. Ethereal music is playing. Bob approaches a bit "out-of-sorts" and then changes to "Mr. Nice Guy" as soon as he realizes where he is and what he is facing.

BOB: *[mumbling, grumbling]* I can't believe this has happened . . . to *me*! At this time! I was just about to close the sale of the century, and this idiot comes sneaking out of his driveway—right in front of my car. I mean, he should have seen me coming. After all, I was doing 65 in a 25 school zone. He at least should have heard my tires squealing around the corner. *I* was the one late for an appointment. Now look where I am. *[approaches the desk]* Oh well, I better make the best of this. Everyone said this place would be better. *[changes voice to be kind and pleasant]* Ah, hello kind angel, is this heaven?

ANGEL: *[kind and gentle]* Yes, it is. Can I help you?

BOB: *[puts on the charm]* I am sure you can. I have a reservation. The name is Slick, Bob Slick. And I will take one of the bigger mansions, if it is finished *[laughs]*, but I can wait a day or two if they don't have all the furniture in.

ANGEL: I'm sorry, Mr. Slick, but I don't have you listed.

BOB: *[shocked]* Wait a minute! What are you talking about? *[rather upset]* There must be some kind of a mistake.

ANGEL: Well, we usually do not make mistakes up here. But I will be happy to look again. *[pages through notebook on the podium]*

BOB: *[begins to sweat and becomes agitated]* Ah, check under that tithe thing. I gave a big gift to that little church on the corner last month. *[tries to help the angel look]* Ah, try under good husband. *[proud]* I was a great husband—to all *three* of my wives. Call them, they will tell you. *[scrambling]* Oh, I know, check under honest . . . never che . . . cheat. . . . Maybe you better try under apologies. I gave a few of those last year. . . . *[panics]* Look, I have to be in that book. I was a nice guy!

ANGEL: I am sorry, Mr. Slick. You are not in the book.

[Freeze, music plays the characters out or go directly to the next scene.]

SCENE 2

Music softly plays as Mrs. Sweetheart approaches the angel at the podium.

IMA: *[walks briskly across the stage, using her cane]* I am so excited. I have waited for this day for years. I can't wait for my new body. It's going to be so good to run and jump and especially to be able to eat popcorn with my own teeth! *[approaches angel very kindly]* Excuse me, I am so sorry to bother you, but I just wanted to let you know, I'm here! *[waves her cane with excitement]* Let the party begin!

ANGEL: I'm sorry, but I don't recognize you.

IMA: Oh, that's okay, honey. You have a lot of people to keep straight. I have plenty of time. I'm not going anywhere. So I'll just wait here while you find my name in your big book. I'm not very strong, but I can help you hold it if you'd like.

ANGEL: Thank you, I can manage. Now what was your name?

IMA: Sweetheart, Ima Sweetheart. That's with an "S," like in sugar.

ANGEL: Let me see, Sweeting . . . Sweetland . . . I'm sorry, Ima . . .

IMA: Here, you can use my glasses. I am sure your eyes are getting tired. You'll find it, just keep looking.

ANGEL: I'm just not finding your name, and our records are really very accurate. . . .

IMA: You can check with my neighbors, the school board, the cashier at the local grocery store. I gave back a nickel that the checkout lady should not have given me—she was new that day—and all my children will tell you that I never missed one of their special days. Now, I don't want to brag, but you should know that I never told a fib, *[emphatic]* not once.

ANGEL: I'm so sorry, Ima.

[freeze; music plays the characters out or go directly to the next scene]

SCENE 3

Ethereal music plays as Jeff approaches the angel at the podium.

ANGEL: *[steps out to greet Jeff]* Jeff, it is so good to see you. We have been expecting you.

JEFF: *[surprised]* You have? But, I thought . . .

ANGEL: Jeff, we have all been celebrating your arrival. Welcome. There are so many people who want to talk to you.

JEFF: Does that mean that I am . . .

ANGEL: In? *[points to book]* Jeff, your name is right here.

JEFF: Really? I can't believe that my name is . . . I mean, . . . after all the garbage in my life . . . the abuse, the damage I caused, the time I was busted, all the lies and games that I played. How in the world—*[looks around]* or in heaven—did I ever get my name in that book?

ANGEL: Jeff, it says right here: February 7, 1998, your name was written in this book. Do you remember that date?

JEFF: February 7? That was the date of my dad's funeral, and a friend talked to me about heaven—this place—and how I could come. *[dawning on him]* I *did* talk to God that day. I invited Jesus into my life, to forgive me of my sins. . . . But that was the last time I talked to my friend, and I have to admit that I haven't talked to God much since that day. But I *can* say that life sure has been different.

ANGEL: Well, Jeff, everything is going to be a whole lot different now.

13

THEME

In 1990 it was reported by the National Census Bureau that 18 percent of all Americans live alone. However, some of the loneliest people in life are those who have "close" family and friends, but close only in a physical or social context. This sketch reveals how lonely people will do anything and everything to be a part of a group.

CHARACTERS

SUSAN: A lonely person. She is dressed in white from head to toe. She carries a purse containing money and a pair of black socks.

BOB: Represents the younger generation. He is dressed in black from head to toe.

BILL: Represents the older generation. He is dressed in black from head to toe. He carries a bag containing an extra-large black sweatshirt and sweatpants.

BETTY: Represents a successful, high-society woman. She is dressed in black from head to toe and carries a large black purse containing a roll of duct tape.

SETTING

Stage left has a bench surrounded by a couple of plants or bushes. Stage right has three stools.

While some music is playing, Susan comes out to stage left and sits on the bench. Bob and Bill come out to stage right and begin to talk and laugh with each other. They are soon joined by Betty, who becomes a part of the conversation. Susan is obviously straining to hear what is being said. The others are working hard to keep her at a distance.

SUSAN: *[forcefully to be heard by the others]* I sure am lonely.

BOB: Did you hear something?

BILL: Not me!

BETTY: I heard absolutely nothing. Nothing at all.

SUSAN: *[cheerfully]* Hi, guys! I'm new in town.

BOB: *[annoyed]* Does anyone know her?

BILL: I don't think so.

BETTY: Who cares? We don't need someone new in our community. *[pause]* Now that we have been rudely interrupted, can we get back to *our* agenda?

BOB: Bill, have you secured the entertainment for our party?

BILL: Bob, it is going to be the best program we have ever had!

[Susan slowly gets up from the bench and moves toward the group, listening with great interest. She does not cross an imaginary line at center stage.]

BOB: Betty, did you contact the caterer?

BETTY: Yes indeed! The food is going to be delectably delightful.

BILL: I am so excited about our party.

BETTY: It is going to be the event of the year. Everyone will be talking about it.

SUSAN: *[interrupts]* Say, I couldn't help but overhear . . . but, could I come?

[The group of three moves into a huddle.]

BETTY: Why, of all the nerve!

BILL: An eavesdropper, if you ask me.

BOB: This new person is rather bold, I would have to say.

SUSAN: I'm sorry, I didn't mean to cause a problem. . . . I was just feeling a little lonely and, being new to the community, . . .

BETTY: Bob, we need to do something about these . . . infiltrators.

BILL: I agree with Betty, we need to stick to our standards.

BOB: Well, what would you suggest?

BETTY: *[pulls the roll of duct tape out of her purse]* Boundaries. We need to establish some boundaries. *[hands the tape to Bob]* Now, gentlemen, you will do *well* to make it clear to this young woman that we are not about to allow the likes of *her* into our prestigious community. Now go on, lay down the line.

BOB: Come on, Bill, give me a hand. *[They stretch the tape across center stage between them and Susan, with the next comment directed sternly at Susan.]* There, that ought to keep the riffraff out.

BILL: *[doubtful]* I don't know, Bob, some people will do *anything* to get into our community. What if they cross that line?

BOB: Bill, we will just have to deal with that when it comes. Until then, let's just finish our plans for the big event!

[Susan goes back to sit on the bench, looking discouraged.]

BETTY: *[looks at the new line on the floor and sees that Susan has retreated to the bench]* Gentlemen, you have done a fine job!

BOB: And both of you have done a fine job with our plans. This is going to be the best annual event we have ever had. I don't think the extra price on the ticket will keep anyone away.

[Susan perks up with interest.]

SUSAN: Excuse me, did you say tickets? *[She reaches in her purse and pulls out some money.]* I would love to buy a ticket. I don't mind paying the extra amount.

BILL: See what I told you? Some people will do *anything* to get into our community.

BETTY: We have words to describe those kinds of people. Ignore her.

SUSAN: *[pleading]* I really want to buy a ticket. Please, may I attend your event?

BOB: *[weakening]* Well, I suppose *one* more isn't going to hurt. I don't suppose she will bother anyone—

BETTY: Oh, Bob, look at her. She is so . . . different! Her clothes are so unlike ours. And who knows where she has been, or what she has done. As far as you know, she could have . . . *[thinks]* an agenda. Yes, she could have an agenda.

BILL: Yeah, Bob. I don't know . . . what if she has an agenda?

SUSAN: *[puzzled]* I don't think I have an agenda. I'm not even sure what an agenda is!

BOB: Look, maybe if we made her more like us. That might make a difference with our "Community Committee." Here, young woman, put these on.

[Bob reaches into a bag and throws to Susan an extra-large black sweatshirt and sweatpants. Susan readily puts them on. The trio stands back looking with a bit of disapproval.]

BETTY: This is not going to work. It is just not acceptable. When are you men going to learn that you can't change people to be like us? We have tried before, and it just doesn't work.

SUSAN: *[pulls out of her purse a pair of black socks and puts them over her white ones]* Hey, guys, please just give me a chance, and I can be just like you. There, now we look alike.

BOB: *[approving]* You did a fine job.

BILL: She *might* pass the "Committee."

BETTY: *[disgusted]* But listen to her language: "Hey, guys." No one will understand her, and, besides, she is still the same underneath all of those . . . garments. *[The others nod in agreement with Betty as Betty folds her arms and turns her back to Susan.]* I say she stays on her side of the line.

SUSAN: *[with growing desperation]* I'm willing to talk differently!

TRIO: *[They look at each other and shake their heads with disapproval.]* No!

SUSAN: What if I don't say a word and if I clean up the mess after the party?

TRIO: *[They look at each other almost approvingly, then quickly switch gears.]* No!

SUSAN: I promise, I promise, I promise! If you let me come just one time, I promise I will never ask again, and if you want me to *[She closes her eyes not to see their possible negative response.]* I will go away and never bother you again.

TRIO: *[confers and reluctantly responds]* Okay, come across the line.

BILL: Hi, my name is Bill.

BOB: I'm Bob.

BETTY: *[cool]* Betty is the name.

SUSAN: Susan, my name is Susan.

TRIO: What?

BILL: She said S . . . S . . . Susan.

BOB: I heard it too.

BETTY: *[fanning herself as if to keep from fainting]* Totally unacceptable.

BOB: Susan, I'm sorry, but your name does not start with a "B" like Bob, Bill, or Betty. It's okay to sound like us and dress like us, but you will have to change your name.

SUSAN: I'm sorry, I can't do that. It is who I am.

TRIO: And we are who we are.

BOB: I'm sorry, Susan, you will have to leave.

[Susan walks away very discouraged; music softly plays.]

BETTY: I told you she was different.

BOB AND BILL: Betty, you were right!

[Trio walks away looking relieved.]

[music crescendos; blackout]

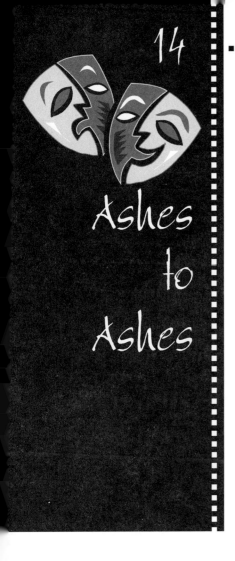

14

Ashes to Ashes

THEME

The Bible tells us that it is appointed for men to die once and after that the judgment, concluding with heaven or hell. But many people do not believe in an eternal destiny.

CHARACTERS

DOCTOR: Mild mannered. He wears a white coat or medical uniform.

WARREN: Late-middle-aged. He is dressed casually.

MARGARET: Warren's spouse of many years. She is dressed casually.

TED: Warren's best friend. He is dressed casually.

SETTING

Scene 1: A table with a few medical items representing a medical office examination room.

Scene 2: A kitchen with table and chairs, a telephone, and a mixing bowl and spatula.

SCENE 1

Warren is buttoning up his shirt and the doctor is looking at his medical chart/clipboard.

WARREN: Well, Doc, what do you think of the San Francisco 49ers? *[pause, tries to get the Doc's attention]* Doc . . . yo, Doc, the 49ers, what do you think?

DOC: *[obviously preoccupied, mumbles with a late response]* Yes, Warren, I wish you were forty-nine. That would be a good age.

WARREN: *[a bit annoyed, now testing the doc]* Doc, so how many combat boots does your mother wear?

DOC: *[still preoccupied]* Ah, three . . . and I was never in combat.

WARREN: *[sarcastic]* Doc, would you like hot fudge or motor oil on your pizza?

DOC: Ah, not fudge, Warren, not fudge.

WARREN: *[yells]* Doc, you haven't heard a word I've said!

DOC: What did you say, Warren?

WARREN: Doc, what is so interesting on that chart? Go ahead, tell me, how many miles do I have left? Will I make it to _____ [Identify a neighboring city] next week?

DOC: Well, it depends on how you are planning to get there.

WARREN: Look, Doc, how long have we known each other?

DOC: About twenty years, Warren.

WARREN: Then give it to me straight, Doc. I'm a big boy. What do your little charts say? Am I going to live, or is this the "big hurrah"?

DOC: Well, Warren, I have good news and . . . bad news.

WARREN: I'll take the good news.

DOC: Welcome to _____ [Name of your program].

WARREN: And the bad news?

DOC: This may be your last one, Warren.

SCENE 2

Dreary music is playing as Warren comes walking toward the kitchen to take a seat. Margaret is talking on the phone and licking a spatula covered with chocolate.

MARGARET: [cheerfully] Yes, Ted, I think I hear him coming up the drive. [licks chocolate] Mmmm. . . . Sure, just come over. I am sure you can borrow Warren's fast-action-double-turbo-hedge-trimmer. Not a problem, Ted. Bye! [a side comment] Men and their toys. [hangs up phone as Warren comes in and takes a seat; Margaret turns to see Warren] Oh, hello dear. . . . [extends spatula to Warren] . . . Here, . . . try this hot fudge I just made.

WARREN: No thanks, babe . . . not . . . hungry.

MARGARET: [trying to be understanding] Oooo, no hot fudge, must have been a bad day on the job?

WARREN: No, in fact, I got another twenty-five-cent raise—

MARGARET: The car! You didn't—not our new car!

WARREN: No, Margaret, the car is just fine.

MARGARET: So, what is all the doom and gloom about?

WARREN: I just saw Jim.

MARGARET: My brother-in-law? Well, you can tell that J-E-R—

WARREN: Save it, Margaret. I saw Jim Murdock.

MARGARET: *[concerned]* Dr. Jim Murdock? What's going on, Warren?

WARREN: Remember that problem I told you about two weeks ago? *[She responds in the affirmative.]* Well, I went to see the doc, and he told me what it is.

MARGARET: *[can't handle this news]* No, no, I don't even want to hear it, Warren. *[She begins to back away, drops spatula.]* Don't you dare tell me those words. *[covers her ears and dashes out]* It is not happening! . . . It is not going to happen.

[Margaret blows right past Ted who walks in at the same time and sees everything coming apart.]

TED: *[to Margaret as she is leaving]* Hey, Margaret, nice to . . . see . . . you. *[to Warren]* Hey, Warren old buddy, let me guess, you are in the D-O-G house. Well, how can I cheer you up, pal? It looks like you just blew it again!

WARREN: Hey, Ted?

TED: Yeah, bud?

WARREN: Do you believe in the . . . hereafter?

TED: Hereafter what? I'm *here after* your fast-action-double-turbo-hedge-trimmer, if that's what you mean—hey, if you don't want me to borrow your little pride and joy I underst—

WARREN: Ted, you know what I mean. . . .

TED: Okay, this is serious, right?

WARREN: About as serious as it ever gets, Ted.

TED: Hereafter? Like in heaven or . . . h . . . h . . . h . . . the hot place?

WARREN: You've got it.

TED: Well, like I heard at my dad's funeral, "ashes to ashes and dust to dust." That's it, pal. That is all there is.

WARREN: But what about eternal life?

TED: What about it?

WARREN: Well, is there any?

TED: How should I know? I've never been there and neither has anyone else to come back and give a report. Hey, if Ted Koppel could do it, he would have had a special on it, and I haven't see the report. So relax, man . . . enjoy life. . . . What are you driving at?

WARREN: So, after this life, I'm not going to see your ugly face or . . . *[serious]* Margaret, or . . . the kids ever again, huh?

TED: Hey, this is as good as it gets, and like everyone says, you only go around once, so "go with all the gusto you can"— you know the verse. Hey, ah . . . where's your turbo-trimmer?

WARREN: It's in the shed, out back.

TED: I'll have it back in an hour. . . . *[melodramatically]* And for my deepest, heartfelt appreciation, I have two tickets for the game next Monday night. What do you say?

WARREN: Thanks, Ted, but I don't think I'll be available next Monday night.

15

A Christmas Eve

THEME

The loss of a loved one or unexpected circumstances can alter our plans and thoughts about Christmas. It is then that we begin to realize what Christmas is all about. Some understand; others do not, as we will see in this sketch.

CHARACTERS

WILCOT JONES: An elderly, unsuccessful owner of a gas station on the outskirts of a small town. He is dressed very poorly with bib overalls, flannel shirt, suspenders, and a stocking cap.

CRAIG JOHNSON: A young, successful businessman stranded by a snowstorm in Wilcot's station. He is dressed in a suit, overcoat, and gloves.

SETTING

The interior of a humble little gas station with a snowstorm outside. A small manger scene, two packages containing gloves and a sweater, and a bag of groceries are needed as props.

Wilcot is sitting on a stool doing a crossword puzzle. A radio (tape player) is playing Christmas music. Craig Johnson comes in out of the storm, stomping his feet and brushing off the snow.

CRAIG: Man, it's cold out there. I could barely see to get in here.

WILCOT: *[never looks up, talks slowly and matter-of-factly]* Worst storm since '78. Need some gas?

CRAIG: *[unkind]* No, I don't need any gas.

WILCOT: Nobody stops here for gas anymore since they put up that new fancy ten-pump convenience place down the road. I can't compete anymore.

CRAIG: Hey, pops, do you have a phone I could use?

WILCOT: Got a phone . . . can't use it.

CRAIG: What do you mean I can't use it?

WILCOT: Doesn't work . . . out of order . . . haven't been able to keep up the phone service this year. Besides, nobody calls here anymore, and I sure don't—

CRAIG: So, where's the nearest pay phone?

WILCOT: Back in town.

CRAIG: But that is . . .

WILCOT: . . . about twelve miles.

CRAIG: I am not going out in that storm again!

WILCOT: Then I guess you're not going to use the pay phone, are you?

CRAIG: Look, I have got to call my wife and kids. They're expecting me. It's Christmas Eve. I have a car full of presents and food to feed an army.

WILCOT: *[into his crossword puzzle]* Seven down. What is a three letter word for "intense happiness and delight" that starts with "J"?

CRAIG: *[answers immediately]* Joy, J-O-Y. . . . Look, is there anything you can do? I've got to get home!

WILCOT: Well, son, I can't fix the weather, and I can't fix the phone. I am not even very good with these crossword puzzles. Sorry, guess I can't help you. . . . But if you need some gas or oil, then I can help you.

CRAIG: Look, I told you I don't need gas or oil. *[pauses, paces, looks out window]* When is that storm going to let up? God forbid that I have to spend Christmas in this dump.

WILCOT: Pardon me?

CRAIG: *[embarrassed]* Ah, . . . nothing, pops . . . nothing. *[pause]* So, what are you doing for Christmas?

WILCOT: I'm doing it.

CRAIG: You're doing a crossword puzzle for Christmas?

WILCOT: You got a better idea?

CRAIG: You're supposed to be with your family or friends, not freezing in this place.

WILCOT: And if I was with my family or friends, then you'd be stranded alongside the road in a blizzard.

CRAIG: So, where is your family?

WILCOT: Mary died two winters ago, and the kids . . . not sure about the kids. They're somewhere . . . I guess.

CRAIG: *[uncomfortable, changes the subject]* Well, at least you have this old heater in the corner. I suppose we could be a lot worse off, huh, pops?

WILCOT: The name is Wilcot. Wilcot Paul Jones, from Georgia.

CRAIG: I'm Craig, Craig Johnson . . . IBM Regional Representative.

WILCOT: *[extends hand to shake]* Well, Craig Johnson, IBM Representative, I guess you're stuck with me for this Christmas.

CRAIG: Yup, . . . here we are. *[looks off, depressed]* Here we are.

WILCOT: You already said that. *[back to crossword puzzle]* Ah, sixteen across. What is a five letter word for "ending quarrels"? *[lets out a bad cough.]*

CRAIG: *[instantly]* Peace. Let's see, P-E-A-C-E. Yeah, that will do it. *[Wilcot coughs again.]* Hey, Wilcot, that is a pretty nasty cough. This cold is going to do you in. You need to have some warmer clothes.

WILCOT: *[coughs, looks out window]* Hey, it looks like the storm is letting up. You might be able to make it, Mr. IBM. Hey, before you leave, I've got something in the back I want to give you.

[Christmas music plays while Wilcot goes in the "back room" and Craig leaves out the front door as if going to his car. He comes back with two packages and a grocery bag. He begins to exit. As Craig exits, he hears Wilcot coming back into the shop. Craig stands outside the door with it slightly ajar and listens to Wilcot.]

WILCOT: *[carries a small manger scene]* Hey, Mr. IBM, I've got a little Christmas present for you and your family. It isn't much, just a little baby and his parents on that first Christmas Eve. It's the story of what Christmas is really all about . . . Craig? . . . *[sees the packages on the counter]* And what is all of this? *[picks up boxes one at a time, reads tags, and opens the boxes]* To Dad, love Craig. *[opens a pair of gloves]* What in the world? These sure will keep my hands warm. *[reads next card]* To Bill, from your brother Craig. *[pulls out a big sweater]* Why of all the . . . *[looks in grocery bag]* He was right, enough food to feed an army or, at least, one old lonely man.

CRAIG: *[goes back in the shop]* Hey, Wilcot, . . . do you know the whole story about that baby and his parents?

WILCOT: Sure do, sonny, sure do.

CRAIG: Then put that sweater on. You're coming home with me. I want my kids to have their Uncle Wilcot share the Christmas story. What do you say?

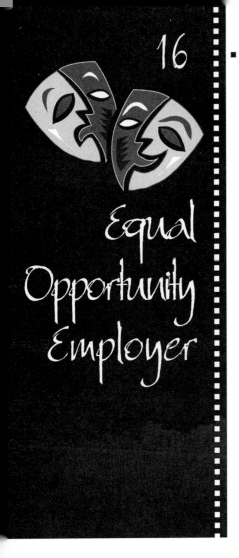

16

Equal Opportunity Employer

THEME

Equal rights are a bit of a misnomer in our society. In this sketch, it is rather obvious that a person's nationality and/or background creates a bias that only leads to social exclusion.

CHARACTERS

JAMES: A friendly but biased, smooth-talking employment counselor. He is wearing a suit.

VICTOR: A not-so-altogether applicant, but he has the right background. His dress is very, very casual, with a baseball cap, etc.

WILLIAM: Well dressed, with a suit and tie, and well qualified for any job, but he has the wrong background.

SETTING

An office with a simple desk, desk chair, and side chair placed stage center. Three side chairs and some magazines are at stage right representing a waiting area. A phone-ring sound effect is helpful.

The three actors come out. James sits at his desk. Victor and William go to the side chairs and begin to read magazines. The phone rings.

JAMES: *[picks up the phone]* Hello, this is the James Houlihan Employment Agency. If you need a job, we will do a job for you, because jobs are our business. This is James speaking, how may I help you? *[pause]* Uh-huh, you are wanting to hire an engineer in electronics. *[making notes]* And it pays $75,000 a year, plus expenses, and benefits, and you want someone right away. . . . Oh, you need two engineers. Well, we will get right on it, Mr. Campbell. The same to you, sir, and thank you for calling.

[Gives his attention to Victor and William seated next to him.] Hello, gentlemen, my name is James Houlihan, and if you need a job, I will do a job for you because jobbing is my business. *[hands them some forms]* Here, fill out these forms and whoever gets done first just come and have a seat for your job interview.

VICTOR: Ah, thank you, Mr. James.

WILLIAM: Yes, thank you, Mr. Houlihan.

VICTOR: *[to William]* Hey, pal, do you have a pen I could borrow?

WILLIAM: *[looks annoyed and hesitates]* Ah, . . . sure. *[offers an extra pen]*

VICTOR: *[leans over to William with application]* Ah, what is this word?

WILLIAM: *[looks at Victor's pointing]* Status. They want to know if you are single or married.

VICTOR: Gee, thanks, you're pretty smart. Why do you think they want to know that? What if, you know, . . . if you are kinda, but not really. You know what I mean, don't you?

WILLIAM: Yeah, sure . . . just put down whatever you think.

VICTOR: *[makes some really busy marks on paper]* There. Finished. Ha, beat you, pal . . . Well, I'm ready! *[Goes up to James]* Here, John.

JAMES: *[with disdain]* The name is James. *[looks at application]*

VICTOR: Hey, I can call you whatever you want. How about "James the man!"

JAMES: James is fine. . . . Ah, you've hardly filled out any of the questions.

VICTOR: Not necessary. I'm qualified for anything. You name it, I can do it.

JAMES: *[very interested]* Is that right?

VICTOR: Sure is . . . I went to Kirby High School in Burkdale.

JAMES: You are kidding! I went to Kirby!

[They both stand and do a silly cheer, with antics.]

TOGETHER: Kirby, Kirby, fight fight fight!

Kirby, Kirby, righty tite mites! Yeah!

JAMES: Wow, a fellow Kirbyite! You know, with a graduating class of twelve, we've got to stick together. Now Victor, let's take a look at your application. Uh-huh, I see you graduated with just less than a one grade point average.

VICTOR: Yeah, I would have done better, but I failed woodshop when I cut the tool bench in half. Not a happy day in my life.

JAMES: I see you have had twelve jobs in the last twelve months.

VICTOR: Like I said, I have a lot of experience.

JAMES: And how is your health?

VICTOR: Not bad, Joe, I just get these really bad headaches.

JAMES: Oh really? When do you get those?

VICTOR: Just when I work, so not too often.

JAMES: Well, thank you, Victor. We Kirby High men must stick together. *[picks up pad from phone notes]* I have a wonderful job for you. How would you like to be an electrical engineer, at a starting salary of $75,000 plus benefits?

VICTOR: *[stands to shake]* I'll take it. An engineer? I love trains!

[Victor exits quickly.]

JAMES: *[realizes he did wrong]* Oh boy. . . . Next.

WILLIAM: Hello, my name is William Hartford, and I want to thank you for the interview. I sure do need a job. That electrical engin—

JAMES: Okay Bill, let me see. *[takes application]* Ah, . . . graduated top of the class at M.I.T. Seven years experience with GM as an . . . electrical engineer. Hmmm . . . married for nine years, two kids, four years in the Marine Corps. . . . Taught at Columbia University in the engineering department. I see . . . hmmm . . . *[shocked]* What? You graduated from Hinckley High School? *[really ripped]* Hinckley High? You guys destroyed our football team in the playoffs in 1985, the score was 54 to 3. You showed no mercy.

WILLIAM: I'm sorry, but I didn't go to the school that year, I was—

JAMES: You Bull Dogs ruined our school year! That was our homecoming game. *[angry]* You Bull Dogs from Hinckley came over to our side of town with that broken-down bus, wearing football uniforms from the Civil War, and with cheerleaders who couldn't jump over a bench, and you bums nailed us to the wall.

WILLIAM: I'm sorry . . .

JAMES: *[sarcastic]* Oh, you're sorry. Well, I'm sorry too. Sorry there are no jobs available for you. You aren't qualified. *You are a Bull Dog*. A Bull Dog! Have you considered the Burger Bin down the road? I heard they're looking for a bus boy.

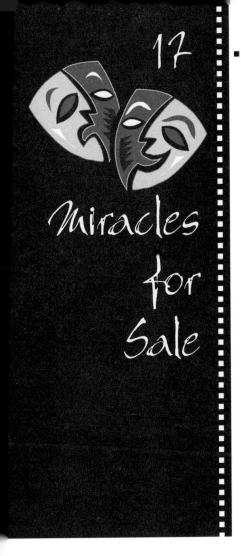

17

Miracles for Sale

THEME

Most people want to see and experience a miracle, especially when they have lost all natural control of their lives and circumstances. In this sketch, our character tries to buy a miracle, only to find that no human company can create, manufacture, or guarantee a real miracle. Only God can do that.

CHARACTERS

BUZ: A young man in hope of purchasing a miracle. Dress is casual.

MONTE: A miracle salesman. He is slick and shrewd as he tries very hard to sell a miracle. He is dressed in a loud, brightly colored sports coat, tie, and plaid slacks.

VOICE: Represents the voice of God.

SETTING

The setting is a table holding several differently sized plain boxes.

Monte comes on stage to straighten out his boxes and get ready for his day of sales. Monte is singing his favorite tune, "I'm in the money." Buz comes walking in the door with a list in his hand.

MONTE: Good day, my boy, good day. Welcome to Miracles Galore, where we guarantee that everything will go your way. Now, what way would you like things to go? Remember our slogan, "Everything's a Miracle!" Monte is my name, now what's your name, boy, and how can I help you?

BUZ: Buz, my name is Buz, and well, I was just looking at my Miracle List—

MONTE: Miracle List? You don't need a list, Buz. Let me suggest our number one selling miracle. *[points to largest box]* It is by far the most popular, especially for a young man like you! Why, it will help you win the lottery. It will give you a promotion. This dandy little miracle will make you rich, boy. It will make you rich! Remember: "Everything's a Miracle!"

BUZ: Wow, that is pretty exciting. *[tries to open up and look in the box]*

MONTE: Not so fast, Buz, not so fast. *[reaches out and prevents Buz from opening box]* This little baby is $99.95; then the miracle is yours.

BUZ: *[a bit discouraged]* Well, that is a lot more than I planned to spend and, besides, that miracle—as nice as it would be—is not on my list.

MONTE: That's not a problem at Miracles Galore where "Everything's a Miracle!" Let me suggest our monthly special. Come here, boy. *[Buz comes close where Monte puts his arm around him "buddy-like."]* You know that little lady you would give anything to go out with? *[trying to act like he knows what is going on]* Ah, . . . the one who is dating your best friend?

BUZ: *[falls into the plan]* Oh, you mean Heather?

MONTE: *[excited]* She's the one . . .

BUZ: . . . and my best friend is Butch Balboa!

MONTE: Monte knows all! *[wipes his brow in relief]*

BUZ: *[nervous]* But, Butch is huge.

MONTE: No problem, Buz, no problem . . . remember our slogan, "Everything's a Miracle" and our monthly special will put old Butch out of business and sweet Heather will be yours.

BUZ: *[excited]* Name your price. *[tries to open up the box]*

MONTE: *[stops him from opening the box]* Just three easy installments of $59.95 and you are on your way. *[holds box tightly]* Would you like me to gift wrap this little miracle for you?

BUZ: Hey, why can't I see these miracles?

MONTE: Then they wouldn't be miracles, Buz. Surprise, the element of surprise, is our special bonus package just for you.

BUZ: *[pulls back, discouraged]* Well, I sure would like to go out with Heather, but I just can't afford these miracles. I didn't think they were going to cost so much.

MONTE: Buz, now you really didn't think that a miracle was cheap, did you?

BUZ: Well, some of my friends said that they just prayed and . . . God brought a miracle.

MONTE: *[laughs cynically]* Then why are you here, Buz?

BUZ: Well, . . . *[looks at list; Monte rolls his eyes, not really listening because he has heard this before]* I have been praying for my sister and she just doesn't seem to get any better, and that has caused my mom and dad to fight a lot, and now they aren't talking to each other, and I did lose my job, and well, my prayers are not getting through. So I thought that maybe you could help me.

MONTE: *[rather conciliatory]* Buz, Buz, "Everything's a Miracle!" at Miracles Galore, *[hands him a very small box]* now just take this introductory miracle . . . only $9.95.

[Buz gives Monte some money and takes the small box with great interest as Monte moves him toward the door.]

BUZ: Now, is this guaranteed?

MONTE: Or your money back! *[Moves Buz out the door and wipes his brow with some relief.]* Oh, this younger generation.

BUZ: *[outside of store, tries to open box but cannot]* I can't seem to get this miracle open. . . . I just didn't realize that they would be this tough and complicated—and expensive. How in the world am I supposed to get this miracle to happen?

VOICE: Buz, have you considered that maybe you and your box *can't* make a miracle happen?

BUZ: *[startled, but slowly looks up]* Whoa, it is you. Hey, how come you haven't talked to me until now?

VOICE: I have been trying to, but you haven't been listening. You had your own ideas of what I was supposed to do and, as you and your box can see, my ways are different from yours.

BUZ: So, what do we do now?

VOICE: Well, for starters, how about giving me your list?

BUZ: But I already talked to you about these things.

VOICE: I know, I heard you, but you didn't *give* me the list. I really want it. *[Buz holds up the list with some reluctance.]* Yes, Buz, I want all of it.

BUZ: Okay, . . . here it is. *[throws list up in the air and it falls]*

VOICE: Great. Now I can get started . . . and the miracles? They will be coming, and you need to watch a little more carefully. They may not be exactly what you expect, but they will be from me. *[Buz tries to speak and voice cuts him off.]* Buz, trust me. And would you do me a favor?

BUZ: Sure . . . anything.

VOICE: Throw that silly box away. *[He does.]* Thanks!

18

Mr. Wisdom

THEME

Some people would like to think that they have all the answers to all the questions in life. Others believe that such all-knowing people exist and are willing to ask questions and trust these "wise" people for the right answers, only to find that the wise of this world are wrong and foolish.

CHARACTERS

MR. WISDOM: A bigger-than-life personality, dressed in a robe, seated high on a platform as if in a judge's stand/bench. He has a very arrogant and rather rude demeanor.

RICHARD: Represents every man with several thought-provoking questions. Dress is casual. He carries a large book.

NANCY: Represents every woman with some very practical questions. Dress is casual.

SETTING

Mr. Wisdom is "perched" high at center stage. His voice is reverberated. Light is hot on the center as the others walk into the lighted area. Everything is rather melodramatic.

Mr. Wisdom marches out in grand procession to find his seat of authority. Richard, carrying a large book, cautiously makes his way to approach Mr. Wisdom.

RICHARD: *[from a distance]* Hello? Hello? Mr. Wisdom, are you there? Hello? It is me, Richard. I have a question.

MR. WISDOM: *[turns toward Richard]* Oh, my, it is you again. I thought I answered all of your questions the last time you bothered me. Well, speak up, what can Mr. Wisdom do for you?

RICHARD: *[humbled]* Mr. Wisdom, if I can beg your pardon . . .

MR. WISDOM: Yes, Mr. Wisdom is pleased that you are begging. Go on, finite one.

RICHARD: Oh, thank you, Mr. Wisdom, and for just a moment of your time . . .

MR. WISDOM: And a moment of my great wisdom and IQ is all that you get. Hurry up.

RICHARD: I have been reading—

MR. WISDOM: Yes, yes . . .

RICHARD: I have been reading in my book of philosophies—

MR. WISDOM: Yes, yes, I probably wrote your book. Keep talking . . .

RICHARD: It says here that we cannot be *absolutely* sure there is a God.

MR. WISDOM: Yes, so, what is your point?

RICHARD: If that is true, Mr. Wisdom, what can we be sure of?

MR. WISDOM: The answer is simple: you can only be sure of what Mr. Wisdom has to say. So, go ahead, ask me another question.

RICHARD: Very well then, what is the purpose of life?

MR. WISDOM: The purpose of your miserable life is to believe everything Mr. Wisdom has to say, because I have all the answers.

NANCY: *[coming in from stage left]* Hello? Excuse me, is anybody there? . . . I am looking for Mr. Wisdom. . . . *[She looks at Richard.]* Oh, hello . . .

RICHARD: *[pleased]* Hello . . .

NANCY: Are you Mr. Wisdom?

RICHARD: I'm . . . sorry, . . . but—

MR. WISDOM: Not him! That idiot knows nothing. Young woman, how could you make such a gross error? *I* am the all-knowing, all-wise man of wisdom and understanding.

NANCY: *[humbled]* Oh, I am so sorry, Mr. Wisdom.

MR. WISDOM: Apology accepted, little one. Now, what do you need from Mr. Wisdom?

NANCY: *[speaks very rapidly]* Well, my name is Nancy, and I was wondering if you could tell me whether I should find a new job or stay at my present one because I am not all that happy at my present job, and if I went to a new job, maybe I would be happy and maybe I wouldn't. *[slows down]* So, could you please tell me what to do?

MR. WISDOM: Nancy, Mr. Wisdom has the answer for you.

NANCY: Oh, I knew you would come through for me.

MR. WISDOM: Of course, Nancy, the answer is: Whistle while you work.

NANCY: Whistle while you work?

RICHARD: But that is what the seven dwarfs did.

MR. WISDOM: Of course, and who do you think told them what to do? Mr. Wisdom kept those short, little, miserable, lazy, sleepy, and dopey guys happy. So, Nancy, do as I say.

NANCY: Well, I suppose I could give it a try. . . .

RICHARD: *[astounded]* I can't believe this! These are the best answers to life's questions?

MR. WISDOM: Mr. Wisdom has all the answers. I beg you to try to find just one person in the universe who has better answers than Mr. Wisdom.

NANCY: *[to Richard]* Well, you know, he really has a point. I mean, you and I are here seeing Mr. Wisdom because no one else answered our questions.

RICHARD: *[to Mr. Wisdom]* Okay, Mr. All-the-Answers, one more question.

MR. WISDOM: *[overly confident]* I can answer every one.

RICHARD: What happens to people when they die?

[Mr. Wisdom begins to squirm.]

NANCY: *[to Richard]* Wow, that is a very good question. I have wondered about that answer for a long time. *[to Mr. Wisdom with a confident directness]* Yeah, I would like the answer to that question, too. What *does* happen to people when they die?

MR. WISDOM: Oh, you low-intelligent beings. Such a simple question. Why, it hardly deserves an answer.

RICHARD: Then humor us, oh great wise one. What is the answer?

NANCY: *[sincere]* Yeah, I really want to know.

MR. WISDOM: *[coughs]* Well, I would say that when a person leaves this planet he goes to another place.

NANCY: And what place would that be, Mr. Wisdom?

MR. WISDOM: Well, it is a place far away . . . a place that is difficult for you simple-minded people to comprehend.

RICHARD: *[strong and direct]* Let's face it. You can't answer the question.

MR. WISDOM: *[offended]* Mr. Richard, excuse me?

RICHARD: I'm sorry, but you can't "whistle" your way out of this one. Admit it. There are some things that you just don't know.

MR. WISDOM: Of all the nerve—

NANCY: Hey, Mr. Richard, you better be careful. What if Mr. Wisdom really does have all the answers?

RICHARD: Look, Nancy, I know I don't know you very well, and you don't know me very well, and I may not have all the answers, but one thing I do know: *[points to Mr. Wisdom] He* is not God.

money:
I Love
It!

THEME

Everyone loves money. We never seem to have enough. We always want more, or so we think. However, when we meet someone who has too much money, our idealized view can change.

CHARACTERS

EMILY: Idealistic with tons of energy. Dress is casual and contemporary.

MEGAN: A little more reserved, but has the same idealistic spirit. Dress is the latest fashion statement.

BOBBY: The guy who appears to have it all. He is perfectly dressed and groomed to meet the highest of wealthy standards.

SETTING

A casual cafeteria set with a long table and chairs.

Megan is sitting eating or drinking as Emily approaches to join her.
Emily is high-spirited and pleased to see Megan.

EMILY: Megan! How are you? Is that a new sweater? [*directly*] Look, girlfriend, have you been holding out on me? That is the third new sweater in three days. . . . It must be nice.

MEGAN: Hi, Emily. It was my birthday last week and, you know, parents, grandparents . . . they all came through with the gift certificates.

EMILY: [*touching and examining sweater*] Gap or J. Crew?

MEGAN: Ah . . . neither.

EMILY: Not . . . Eddie Bauer?

MEGAN: Please, Emily, give me a little more credit and class than that. . . .

EMILY: Ooops, sorry. . . . Abercrombie?

MEGAN: Bingo! New store in the mall—we finally got one.

EMILY: Wow, I need more birthdays.

MEGAN: Hey, were you in third-hour psych class?

EMILY: With psycho Prof. Peters? That guy is wacko. Where is he coming from?

MEGAN: Got me! He got pretty religious today.

EMILY: Aren't there laws against him talking about all that God stuff?

MEGAN: I sure wish he would keep his personal opinions to himself.

EMILY: Amen. I mean, who is he to say that having *[looks and touches the new sweater]* new things is going to mess us up?

MEGAN: I don't know. And did you hear that line about loving money is the root of all evil?

EMILY: *[laughs]* I know. . . . Where does he get that stuff? The guy is out of the stone age. "A new sweater a day" is my motto.

MEGAN: With matching slacks . . .

EMILY/MEGAN: Amen! *[They high five each other.]*

MEGAN: What are you going to do when you get out of this place?

EMILY: Make lots of money. What else?

MEGAN: Well, you could marry someone with lots of money. That would be a whole lot easier.

EMILY: Ah, too controlling. Then you have to say "yes sir" and "no sir." *[with certainty and clarity]* I want to be my own person and be controlled by *no one*.

MEGAN: *[off in her own little dream world]* Give me a rich boy and I will have *it made*.

EMILY: *[off in her own little dream world]* Give me my own company and I will have *a* maid.

MEGAN: I will never work a day in my life.

EMILY: Everyone will work for me and that is *the* life.

MEGAN/EMILY: *[dreamy]* Money, money, and more money!

MEGAN: Well, it's a nice thought. What are you doing for spring break?

EMILY: *[disgusted]* My parents are taking me and my brother on a fishing trip.

MEGAN: Not in a *cabin?*

EMILY: With an outhouse!

MEGAN: Oh, Emily, how will you ever survive?

EMILY: I'm not sure, Megan. Just the thought of touching a dead fish is enough to send me through the roof. So, what are you doing during break?

MEGAN: Mom has us going to the farm to see my grandma again.

EMILY: Whoopee, but it beats a canoe.

MEGAN: You have never had a wet kiss from my grandma.

EMILY: You have never been canoeing with my dad.

MEGAN: At least you don't have to visit cousins and listen to aunts fuss all over you like you are six years old.

EMILY: Anything is better than mosquitoes, a sleeping bag, and Dad's hunting stories around a camp fire.

MEGAN/EMILY: We're doomed!

MEGAN: *[looking off to stage right]* Oh my gosh, here comes Bobby Wingate.

[Bobby enters and approaches the girls.]

EMILY: Of Wingate Motors?

MEGAN: He is so rich.

EMILY: He drives a Ferrari.

MEGAN: His dad owns three malls.

EMILY: That would be heaven.

MEGAN: Dating Bobby?

EMILY: No, silly, owning three malls.

BOBBY: Hi guys, can I join you?

MEGAN: *[losing herself]* For life. . . .

BOBBY: Pardon me?

MEGAN: *[catches herself]* I . . . I mean . . .

EMILY: *[covering]* She means "knife" . . . she needs to borrow a knife.

BOBBY: No problem. You can borrow mine.

EMILY: So, Bobby, what are you doing for spring break?

BOBBY: I think we're going to one of our vacation homes.

MEGAN: Is it a cabin? Emily and her family are—*[Emily takes a napkin and sticks it in Megan's mouth.]*

BOBBY: No, it's in Cancun.

EMILY: What a dream.

BOBBY: Actually, it's a real pain.

MEGAN: Excuse me?

BOBBY: It's boring. We go every year. Sit in the sun, swim in the ocean, eat food that you can't pronounce or identify, then come back home.

MEGAN: *[dramatic]* Oh, to be bored . . .

EMILY: . . . just for a moment.

BOBBY: *[very sincerely and matter-of-factly]* You know, I hear of families going on vacations to grandparents' farms and going on camping trips, making fires, catching fish, and, you know, *[girls shake their heads negatively]* that must be a wonderful time.

EMILY: What you talking about, Bobby?

BOBBY: Really. Our family just goes to an island or Europe, my parents do their thing, and they expect me to enjoy it while I sit by a pool or eat dinner in a restaurant . . . alone. Not much fun.

MEGAN: But I thought that Cancun and France and everywhere else was . . .

BOBBY: Wonderful? No thanks. I would love to just have a family thing sometime with just us—no other people and no props to entertain us. But I guess that will never happen. *[looks at watch]* Well, I didn't mean to get so personal . . . sorry . . . I need to get to my next class.

[Bobby exits.]

MEGAN: Whoa. . . . Maybe grandma's kisses aren't all that bad.

EMILY: And Dad's goofy stories *are* kind of funny. But I ain't touching a fish.

20

Angels Come from K-Mart

THEME

Angels have become a rather popular theme over the last few years. However, it appears that most people do not understand where angels come from, or why they were created by God. This sketch raises some good questions about God's angelic beings.

CHARACTERS

ANGIE: A little girl who asks lots of good questions. She is about seven years old. Dress may include a dress, pigtails, and large freckles.

MALLORY: A good mom to Angie, who gives rather unusual answers . . . or, actually, very usual answers to Angie's questions. She is a little "cheesy." Dress is casual.

GORDON: Angie's dad, who is always in the doghouse. His dress is very casual.

SETTING

A small Christmas tree should be stage center. It is in the process of being decorated by Angie and her mom.

Christmas music, such as "Hark, the Herald Angels Sing," is played while Angie and her mom come out to the stage carrying a box or two of tree decorations including an angelic tree topper. They put decorations on the tree while they dialogue.

ANGIE: Hey, Mommy?

MALLORY: Yes, sweetheart.

ANGIE: Why do we have a Christmas tree in our house?

MALLORY: *[pauses to think of a good answer]* Well, because . . . all the neighbors have a tree and we want to keep the neighbors *happy* at Christmas . . . and that is keeping the Christmas spirit. *[really satisfied]* Yes, that is what Christmas is all about.

ANGIE: *[holding an angelic tree topper ornament]* Mom?

MALLORY: Yes, Angie.

ANGIE: Why do we put angels on top of Christmas trees?

MALLORY: Well . . . [thinks a moment] Well, because . . . the Johnsons . . . and the Smiths . . . and the Griswolds . . . and the Bells and the Browers and the Dobsons all have angels on the tops of their Christmas trees.

ANGIE: [still holding and looking at the angel] Moms?

MALLORY: [just a little annoyed] Yes, Angie?

ANGIE: Where do angels come from?

MALLORY: [without hesitation] K-Mart, sweetie . . . aisle seven.

ANGIE: K-mart invented angels?

MALLORY: Well, you finally got me there. I guess I don't really know where they come from.

ANGIE: Well, Tommy Murphy said they fly to earth from heaven to tell people good stuff in their dreams, but they are not really real like the *Touched by an Angel* TV show. So, are angels like pretend human birds?

MALLORY: Well, I guess that is true . . . sort of. . . . Well, to be honest, honey, I have never seen a real angel.

ANGIE: [a little excited] Wow, Mom, you mean there are real angels to see?

MALLORY: [seems sure, but then doubts herself] Of course! . . . I think. . . . Well, maybe they are not real . . . like you and I are real. . . . Maybe they are more like—

ANGIE: The tooth fairy? Are they kind of like the tooth fairy who brings you three quarters when you lose a tooth and puts them under your pillow?

MALLORY: [stops what she is doing] Wait a minute, you only got seventy-five cents for that last tooth?

ANGIE: [pleased] I put the three quarters in my bank.

MALLORY: [to herself] Why that tightwad. . . . Wait until your father gets home. . . .

ANGIE: Why Mom? Does Daddy know the tooth fairy? Cause if he does, maybe he knows an angel.

MALLORY: [a bit cynical] Your father is going to need an angel for protection.

ANGIE: Is that like a guardian angel?

MALLORY: Speaking of guardian angels . . . I think I just heard your father safely drive in the garage.

ANGIE:　Good, maybe Daddy can tell me all about angels.

GORDON:　*[happy]* Hey, there are my two favorite decorators!

ANGIE:　Hi, Daddy!

MALLORY:　*[jumps right on him]* Save the nice-guy routine you . . . tightwad.

GORDON:　Hey, do I detect a little . . . frustration?

ANGIE:　Yeah, Mom is having a hard time describing angels, but she said you know the tooth fairy and maybe you know some angels.

MALLORY:　*[to Gordon off to the side]* I gave you six quarters for her tooth last week. What happened, tooth fairy friend?

GORDON:　Well, I ah . . . I was a little short for the pop machine at work . . . and I sort of . . .

ANGIE:　Daddy?

GORDON:　*[more than happy to switch gears]* Yes, princess?

ANGIE:　Daddy, do you know any angels?

GORDON:　Only your mother . . . and a California baseball team.

ANGIE:　No, you know what I mean. Are angels real?

GORDON:　Well, they are as real as you want them to be.

ANGIE:　But that is just in pretend land. Where did Harold's angels come from?

GORDON:　Ah, Harold's angels?

ANGIE:　Yeah, like the Christmas song, *[singing]* "Hark the Harold's angels sing, glory to the newborn king." You know, when baby Jesus was born.

GORDON:　*[trying to be kind, but authoritative]* Ah, that story was told a long time ago . . . and no one has seen any real angels since, so I don't think that angels are really all that real.

ANGIE:　Daddy?

GORDON:　*[a little nervous]* Yes, dear.

ANGIE:　If angels aren't real in the Bible story, then maybe baby Jesus isn't real either.

GORDON: Mallory, do we have anything else we can put on the top of the tree?

MALLORY: Yeah, but it will cost you three quarters.

21

Here Today, Gone Tomorrow

THEME

Life is short, too short. We all wish we had more time in each day, in each year, and in each lifetime. But it is appointed for men to die once and after that the judgment. So, the question is, how are we spending today? This sketch reveals that today does count because we may not have tomorrow.

CHARACTERS

WENDELL: A late-middle-aged man. He is frazzled as he deals with everyday problems. He wants to be in control, but hard as he tries, he fails. He is dressed semi-casually.

LARRY: Wendell's carefree and casual son. A poor relationship with his father is obvious. He is casually dressed in jeans and a jacket in any color but red.

MALCOLM: The death angel, dressed in a white sweat suit or an all white outfit.

SETTING

A home office with a desk and chair, phone, etc., downstage center. A smoke machine would be ideal, as suggested in the script, but not needed.

Wendell is talking on the phone trying to make a deal with his banker. He is obviously upset and just about out of control as he begs for a break.

WENDELL: *[very dramatic]* Look, just one more month. I've got the deal of the century lined up to close at the end of the month. I am going to make a bundle, and then I can get caught up on the mortgage and pay off our insurance account. *[pleading]* I just need one more month . . . four small weeks . . . twenty-eight little days. . . . *[nearly crying]* Please give me some time . . . just a little time. . . .

LARRY: *[carefully approaches his strung-out father]* Hey . . . ah, Dad? Dad, can I talk to you a second?

WENDELL: *[still on the phone]* Hello? Hello? *[slams down receiver and barks at his son]* What do you want? Why do you always interrupt me when I am on the phone?

LARRY: Because you are always on the phone. Sorry, Dad . . . I didn't mean to disturb you. . . .

WENDELL: *[mocks him]* Didn't mean to disturb you. . . . Then why did you? You can be the most inconsiderate kid, always thinking of yourself. Well, what do you want this time?

LARRY: Well, I was just wondering—

WENDELL: *[yells to offstage wife]* Helen, where is that cup of coffee I asked for ten minutes ago? Helen!

LARRY: Dad, Mom is taking care of Sandy's knee. She fell off the porch.

WENDELL: Always something else. Your mother always has time for everyone but me. Now what is it you want?

LARRY: I was wondering if I could have the car to go to _____ *[insert name of your program].*

WENDELL: I suppose you're going out with those deadbeat friends of yours?

LARRY: *[firm]* Dad, you don't even know my friends. You are always too busy making your . . . deals. Look, forget I even asked.

[Larry starts to walk away, upstage.]

WENDELL: *[not even looking at him]* Boy, don't walk away from me like that.

LARRY : *[deliberately]* Why, Dad? You will forget in twenty seconds or as fast as you can make your next phone call that I was even here. I'll bet you don't even know what color my jacket is.

[Larry exits.]

WENDELL: *[yells]* Helen, bring me that coffee! *[picks up phone, starts dialing]* Hello. Order department. *[sarcastic]* Yes, I can hold. *[sits back in chair]* Red . . . the boy's jacket was red! *[yells]* Helen, where is that . . . *[grabs chest, coughs with great pain—smoke machine begins, music plays—as he passes out in his chair and uses his last breath]* coffee!

[Malcolm appears through the fog, speaking kindly.]

MALCOLM: Wendell . . .Wendell . . . *[touches Wendell to awaken him]* Wendell, it is time.

[Wendell wakes up.]

WENDELL: Huh? What? Who . . . who are you? What is going on here? Look, pal, I can't talk to you right now, I need to make a few calls here to save my business, and my home, and my . . . family. Call me for an appointment.

MALCOLM: *[points to phone and stuff on desk]* Wendell, I don't think any of that is necessary anymore. But go ahead and try one more call if you would like.

WENDELL: *[tries to make a call]* The phone is dead. *[yells]* Helen, where is my cup of . . . *[begins to realize something is wrong]*

MALCOLM: *[kindly]* I'm sorry, but Helen cannot hear you.

WENDELL: *[a bit stunned]* Are you telling me I am—

MALCOLM: Face it now or later.

WENDELL: But I can't be dead. I have way too much to do. Check your calendar. You guys made a mistake, that's all. Now just send me back.

MALCOLM: I'm sorry, Wendell, but that is not within my power. I am simply here to take you to your new home.

WENDELL: Are you the . . . the . . . death angel?

MALCOLM: Well, I prefer to be called Malcolm. That is my name.

WENDELL: Listen, let me make you a deal.

MALCOLM: Sorry, no deals allowed. I have strict orders to take you with me.

WENDELL: Listen, we are talking about a long time up there, right?

MALCOLM: That is true. . . . Eternity is forever.

WENDELL: So, what can just a few more days hurt down here? I have got to take care of . . . *things.*

MALCOLM: You should have thought of those things earlier.

WENDELL: *[humored]* Oh, I get it . . . this is a dream and when I wake up, I will be nicer to Helen, spend more time with my son—and his deadbeat friends—and be a little more honest with my business. *[closes and opens eyes]* Okay, I'm awake now.

MALCOLM: Wendell, this is not a dream.

WENDELL: Look, Malcolm, or whoever you are, did Helen hire you to come in here and do this? *[yells]* Okay, Helen, nice trick. The game is over . . . and you don't have to bring me that cup of coffee, Sweetheart.

MALCOLM: *[looks at Wendell with his arms folded]* We need to go now.

WENDELL: But I need more time. I need more time. Look, I will even read my Bible and pray and study *theology* . . . anything, just name it.

MALCOLM: *He* is ready for you.

WENDELL: All right, . . . but how about just one last phone call?